IGNITII
SUCCESS
BEYOND
BELIEFS

How to get
from where you are
to your greatest yet to be

Juliet Vorster

SpiritUs Publishing

Copyright © 2014 by Juliet Vorster

First Edition

Second printing

ISBN: 978-0-9928243-0-3

Written by Juliet Vorster
Printed and bound in the UK by printdomain.net
Cover design concepts by Paul Scadding
Front cover background created by Tiana
Published by SpiritUs Publishing

To Janet and Jack Vorster, thank you for
enabling me into the spiralling vortex
of my greatest yet to be.

To my beloved Mary,
thank you for remembering
in the moments I forget, LNB.

Dearest Sylvia,
You are brighter than 10,000
Suns. Let your light shine,
and trust yourself.
All my love
Juliet
X

CONTENTS

PRAISE FOR THIS BOOK

"Juliet is a powerhouse of positivity, radiating with love from her most humble and gracious heart. To use the word 'inspirational' could not possibly do this book justice. Juliet has truly captured the very essence of our human experience and delivered a book that enlightens the spirit in each reader.

Whether you're brand new to this subject or a master with many years of practice, this book encompasses comprehendible ideas and simple techniques to guide you along your journey. And the best part...they're all tried and tested measures by which Juliet genuinely lives the life of her dreams by."

~ Luke Wright, Writer & People Person

"The bad news: people who don't deliberately develop their beliefs about their worth rarely sustain financial success.

And the good news: Juliet Vorster has a practical, powerful system for you to discover your value... and never go back! Juliet shares and teaches from a spiritual maturity that will inspire you to greater success in every area.

This book is a gem."

~ Karen Russo

Award-winning author, The Money Keys: Unlocking Peace, Freedom and Real Financial Power

"Juliet - your book, Igniting Success Beyond Beliefs, is a wonderful and valuable treasure. We are blessed by its valuable content. Much love!"

~ David Ault, Singer, Author, Humanitarian

"The title of the book you are holding is of course, Igniting Success Beyond Beliefs. That title could as well be the summation, because at the end of your journey through these pages you will have discovered that your old belief systems have been a wet blanket on the brilliant flame of your true potential."

~ Rick Nichols, Author and Story Teller

"Whether you are already on a personal growth path or looking for some inspiration and ideas to make positive changes to your life, this book has something for everyone. Juliet walks her talk and her passion and enthusiasm is not only genuine but infectious.

There are hidden gems and insights at every turn of the page but you will gain the most from this book if you're prepared to put in some work and do the exercises and practises. They are easy to follow and implement and at times fun too. Juliet will guide you through them all with sensitivity and an understanding for what you're going through, as she's used them all herself.

Juliet's greatest desire in life is to help as many people as she can to live the life that's their birthright - thriving, joy-filled and abundant. So, if you're ready and willing to let go of your old, limiting thoughts and beliefs you too can 'Ignite Success Beyond Beliefs' and start living the life you thought you could only dream of."

~ Nicky Jennings, Transformational Nutritional Coach

"With a unique blend of examples, humor, spiritual messages, and research, this book takes you on a journey to understand how your beliefs have impacted your life up until now. You will be inspired with the possibilities for creating new and wonderful experiences. This is a book you can read many times and continue to get valuable insights for your life."

Patricia J. Crane, Ph.D., author "Ordering from the Cosmic Kitchen"

ACKNOWLEDGEMENTS

Although my name is on the cover as the author, this book could not have happened without many seen and unseen helpers. I could fill many pages with long lists, so I apologise if I have forgotten anyone.

I am deeply grateful to everyone I have met on my journey so far. Each one of you has touched me, and helped me to become the person I am today. Thank you.

I would not have written this book had it not been for Patricia Crane, Phd. Patricia was my first teacher in this arena. Her patience, guidance and love continue to be a wonderful support and I greatly appreciate her presence in my life. Patricia is ably supported by her wonderful husband, Rick Nichols, who has also been a jewel in my treasure box of transformation. Thank you both for all your compassion, kindness and love.

On a very practical level, this book would be much less than it is without the guidance of Dennis Merritt Jones. His direction, clarity and wisdom were essential elements in creating the finished product. Dennis, a simple 'thank you' is vastly insufficient in expressing the gratitude I have for our journey together. I look forward to more grand adventures in the perfect moment of now.

I also send out great gratitude to the following people: To Teresa and David, for getting me started on this journey by introducing me to Louise Hay and her book *You Can Heal Your Life.* To Alison Lamb, for being a guinea pig for these pages. To Tiana for letting me loose with her artwork. To Paul Scadding for creating inspirational concepts for the book cover. To my editor, Jane Goodfellow, whose attention to detail inspires me to greater things. To Terry Cole Whittaker, for seeing something within me that I could yet see for myself. To Anya Slater for being such a patient and compassionate teacher.

I would not have gained the knowledge and experience to write this book without all the clients, students, teachers and mentors that I have been blessed to share this mysterious journey with. Whilst there are too many to list individually, I send out my sincere appreciation to each one of you for your willingness and your presence.

Finally, thank you Mary for being my support system, my sounding board, and for being willing to read it all 'one more time'. I could not have done it without you.

FOREWORD

You were born hardwired for success. If your current life does not reflect your "idea" of success you might recoil at this statement, but it is nonetheless true. This is because success is a universal principle that is imbued in all living things. You need look no further than nature and you'll see the principle of success operating flawlessly. The same universal principle that makes a weed successful at being a weed also works to a make a rose successful at being a rose; the universal principle of success is entirely neutral and non-preferential - it is predisposed to assist *every* living thing to succeed according to its own inherent programing. In this context, we, as individuals, cannot _not_ be successful—the question is, how are you "programmed" to use the principle of success? The difference between you, the weed, and the rose is that a weed can never become a rose because its DNA (programing) is structured to be a weed. Unlike the weed and the rose, your emotional and mental DNA (programing) is modifiable—it can be "updated" so to speak. This means you can consciously use the principle of success in new and creative ways that enhance your life because you have a thinking mind which can transcend its own preconditioned beliefs; it can update its own programing. In other words, you can choose to harness and redirect the principle of success in a manner that transforms your life. That is what Juliet Vorster's book is about; directing this universal principle of success in a new way—a conscious way—and igniting your success based on a deepened understanding of your current beliefs and how to change them.

You are a living organism and, as such, the Universe has "installed" the principle of success at the center of your being. Just as the invisible life force within the stem of a rosebush naturally pushes out, manifesting as a beautiful rose, the human life *must* also express —it *must* push out. In other words, your life contains unconditioned and unrealized potential until it pushes out and becomes personalized and manifested by means of you and your deepest beliefs (programing). You were born hardwired for success and in this you have no choice—you are a success now, even if that success is currently not to your liking; you are succeeding at manifesting at the current level of your programing. The question then is, do you wish to succeed in new ways, ways which affirm your highest and greatest potential? In this you *do* have a choice. There is something within you that already knows the answer to that question and that is why you have picked up this book. A new paradigm for living awaits you if you are ready to do your part. Yes, you have a role to play in creating the life that lies beyond your current beliefs, your current programing. In reading this book you'll discover a power within that will enable you to identify and challenge even your deepest hidden beliefs that have kept you from succeeding at "succeeding" in life affirming ways.

The good news is you have chosen to take this journey of transformation with a master teacher. Juliet Vorster is one of the clearest thinkers I know and she is fully committed to what she teaches; she not only talks the talk, she walks the walk. The principles Juliet teaches will enrich every area of your life *beyond* what you currently can conceive of - if you use them. The principles she has mastered are not exclusively hers; they are as ancient as time - but she has done the heavy lifting required to embody the principles, making them her own in such a manner that has enabled her to speak as an authority on successful living. Juliet speaks with an authentic voice; she is transparent, passionate, wise beyond her years, joyful, and has a sense of humor that will make the journey through this book a pleasure. At the end of each chapter you'll find powerful practices and tools to help you reshape and redirect the energy of the principle of success. You'll discover that Juliet not only points the way to igniting success in your life beyond your current beliefs, she takes the journey with you in a very personal way.

There are no mistakes. This book has called to you at this time because you are now ready to succeed in life in an entirely new way. The only thing required of you is a willing intention to step into the limitless possibilities that lie waiting for you just beyond your current beliefs of what is possible. It is then and there that you can name and claim the dream that has been waiting for you to come true. Follow your guide Juliet - she knows of what she speaks. Igniting your success is a given when you know how. Do *you* believe it? And so it is and shall be.

Peace,

Dennis Merritt Jones

Award winning author of, The Art of Being - 101 Ways to Practice Purpose in Your Life, and The Art of Uncertainty - How to Live in the Mystery of Life and Love It

www.DennisMerrittJones.com

Foreword

INTRODUCTION

"A mind is a terrible thing to waste."

This quote from the United Negro College Fund, used as an advertising slogan back in the 1970s, inspired a rapper named Gary Byrd to incorporate it into his song called "The Crown" which he performed with his group 'The GB Experience'. The lyrics, which I remember from my early rap and hip hop dancing days, have always stayed with me and have somehow helped to steer me through the sticky floors and untied laces of my life. They have been a constant reminder to me that I am more than I think I am, and I can - in any moment - consciously decide what to think and what to believe.

You too, are more than you think you are. In this book you will learn some new things about your powerful mind. You will learn how to use it to achieve the success you desire in life. You will learn that, regardless of any experience you have had which may have taught you that you are somehow 'destined' to poverty, lack, failure, pain, rejection, addiction or abandonment, you were born thriving, happy and successful.

You will learn that the negative things you think and believe about yourself and life are simply not true, and you were not born thinking or believing them. Best of all, you will learn that through the regular application and practise of simple tools and processes you can change the way you think and rewire your brain, and by doing so, experience a life of fulfilment, joy, abundance, peace and love.

The power of words

There are a few words and phrases I want to explain before we get started. In the title and pages of this book I refer to your "greatest yet to be". This is a phrase I have coined which speaks to the ever-unfolding experience of living that is always spiralling upward, just like a reverse helter-skelter. Every one of us is on a journey in our physical bodies, although I believe we are much more than the carbon atoms that make up our physical existence. Along the way, as we experience different events, we learn more about ourselves and life. This knowledge constantly takes us into our greatest yet to be over and over again. Every time we step into the next level, there is always another level to rise into.

It's a strange paradox that we are simultaneously whole and perfect and always in the process of becoming more. Our journey, to me, is like peeling a gigantic onion. To paraphrase Donkey in the first Shrek movie, we're complicated things, with many layers. When we finally peel away the last layer of an onion, we get to nothing (literally, 'no thing'). There isn't a stone or core, there is just the final layer - then the onion ceases to exist. All the layers have been transformed. Similarly, I believe that when we have peeled and transformed all the layers of this particular human existence, we get to leave and return to the infinite energy from which all things come, including us.

I will also talk about consciousness a great deal. For me, consciousness is the sum of every experience, thought and belief that I have ever had. It is not a fixed thing. It is something that is constantly changing and expanding as we have new life experiences and as we think new thoughts. Each one of us has our own individual consciousness which also feeds into the collective consciousness. This collective consciousness of humanity feeds into the Universal Mind, which is the all-knowing intelligence from which everything is created. Every thought, belief, invention and experience exists in the universal energy of the collective consciousness. Everything that ever is, was, or will be, is known in the Universal Mind. You may not know this, but you have constant access to this Mind. You probably already use it regularly without even knowing it.

Just like working on your phone, pad or computer, you have a choice to connect to the internet or not. Sometimes you don't need all the answers that search engines have to offer, and sometimes it's really helpful to 'Ask Jeeves'. In exactly the same way, you can 'ask' the Universal Mind. Have you ever been struggling to find a solution for a problem, gone to sleep, and then awoken the next morning with an inspired idea that resolves everything? Or have you pondered some deep esoteric question about life, only to have a friend randomly start a conversation on the very same subject and offer their experience from something they had just learned? We are all connected to this infinite intelligence. Our asking comes simply from thinking and feeling. As I mentioned just now, we are so much more than the carbon of our bodies - we are energy, operating in a much bigger pool of energy. When we seek answers, we energetically, and subconsciously, ask questions of the Universal Mind, and sooner or later we will get answers. It's a bit like the Borg Collective, only less intrusive and on a universal scale. (If you don't understand this analogy, please find a Star Trek fan and ask for an explanation, or, somewhat similar to the Universal Mind, you can always ask Wiki.)

This book is not about how to create or manifest 'things' but it will teach you how to change your belief system so that you can create the life you want. It will also explain why manifesting is science and not magic. It is a book that is designed to totally change the way you think. It is not telling you what to think but instead invites you to change how you think.

This book is an invitation to you to do more than simply read another personal transformation book. It is an invitation to "JFDI" (just flipping do it). To move beyond reading and wishing, and instead move to taking action and making changes so that you see the results. Although I have no attachment to you taking the action I invite, I sincerely and passionately hope you do. This book is written from my experiences, from things I have already applied in my life, that have enabled me to utterly transform my entire life experience. That's why I'm so passionate about what I teach. I know, without a shadow of a doubt, that if you will say, "Yes!" to the invitations issued through these pages, if you will take the challenge of creating new practices and believing new things, then you will change your life for the better and you will enter the spiralling vortex of your greatest yet to be.

And let me tell you, no matter what you are currently thinking, you are worthy and deserving of a spectacular life. Yes, You!

Chapter 1

FIRM FOUNDATIONS
ARE ESSENTIAL

"Perseverance is the foundation of all actions."

~ Lao Tzu

I believe the old adage that 'life is a journey, not a destination', and I do my best to live by it. I am human, however, so there have been occasions when I've completely forgotten this truth. There have been many times when it has felt like I have unconsciously stopped my own journey of growth and learning. In the early days it wasn't so much a stop as a crashing and crumbling. Those crashes most often happened because I didn't have any foundations, firm or otherwise. I was bouncing from one quick fix or shiny object to another, not realising that I needed to build the structure of my life on firmer ground if it was to sustain me through the journey.

When I recently started thinking a little deeper about the idea of foundations and the need to build lasting support, I had a valuable new insight: I realised that, when it comes to physical buildings, your location in the world makes a difference to the physical foundations you need in order to create a structure that will last. My friends in California build their houses to withstand earthquakes. In Edmonton, Canada, most houses are built to withstand the cold and snow; and in rural Thailand most houses are built up on stilts to withstand the floods. I could cite other locations, all with their own special needs when it comes to building construction. This is valuable information for the building of houses, but when it comes to building a firm foundation for our lives, I believe we can all use a similar design and construction method.

I am writing this book from an English house built in the 1930s, which means the house is already in its 80s. I expect it to keep going for at least another 100 years (although probably not with me in it). The house has firm foundations and is constructed in a proven method that works well in this geographical location. When we think about creating foundations for our lives we need to take a similar approach to those 1930s builders in that we need to build something lasting, that will see us through the journey of our life - mentally, emotionally, physically and spiritually. If we don't, then as I have already discovered, we crumble, and fall into disrepair quite easily. It's not just about creating foundations that allow you to survive the journey - it's about creating foundations that allow you to live a thriving life. A life in which you feel successful, joyous, abundant, appreciated, fulfilled and loved.

Take a nice, deep breath right now. Think about the current foundations of your life. Are they strong and solid, yet flexible and fluid enough to sustain you through a long and happy life? Perhaps you have some areas where you answer yes, and some where you're not so sure. Wherever you are right now, it's good to have a reference point to start from. That way you can be more mindful as you expand your awareness and knowledge through the journey in this book.

Foundations, principles and practise

Being a diligent student and researcher, I set off to discover what the dictionary had to tell us about the word 'foundations'. Of all the things I read, the two descriptions that most captured my imagination were these:

a. the idea that a foundation is 'the lowest load-bearing part of a building', and

b. that a foundation is the underlying principle upon which other concepts are built.

I love both these descriptions because they jointly support my concept that our foundational beliefs and understandings bear the load of our lives and form the basic principles upon which we construct our experiences. When we have poor foundations, there is very little to help us withstand the really big challenges that sometimes land in our laps. That is when we may find ourselves crushed by the weight of everyday life. Anxiety, stress, worry, and even depression can sometimes be the physical result. To avoid any form of collapse and to create a solid base that will sustain the ever-evolving structure of our life, it is good to first create a blueprint, or design, for what we want.

One of my great passions is facilitating transformation for people regardless of what their life has looked like in the past. I will mention it over and over through this book; these concepts apply universally. It doesn't matter who you are, what your past looks like, how old or young you are today, what you have done, what colour your skin is, where you were born, or any other 'thing' we humans use to mistakenly divide ourselves from each other. A new blueprint can be created at any time. It is never too late to sit down and start designing your life the way you want it to be.

An architect uses known physical laws and principles to create a design and build a structure. There are similar laws and principles that apply to our lives. And just like the architect, we can use them to create strong foundations, and build lasting structures for our successful, thriving lives. As we journey together through these pages you will learn more about these laws and principles. You will also learn practical ways to apply them in your life so that you can ignite success beyond beliefs.

How much time have you put into thinking about the bigger picture for your life? I don't mean goal-setting for specific external achievements. I'm talking about higher intentions for how you want to feel, the kind of difference you want to make and the nature of the relationships you want to have, both with yourself and others. It's time to become the conscious architect for your life.

There comes a time, in every project, when the design is ready and the building work must start. However, before we start building, we must clear the land. Just like any building project, we don't simply show up and start digging the footings in amongst the weeds and rubble of what was there before. First we must survey the site, clear the existing debris and level the land, so that our foundations create the best possible load-bearing base to support our subsequent building.

The land that we are preparing in this book is your mind, or consciousness. Together we will clear a space through the clutter of what has gone before and make ready the ground of your understanding upon which we will build new foundations. These foundations take the form of universal principles that provide structure as well as a firm base for living a happy, successful and thriving life.

You are so much more than you think

Every thing that was ever created by a person had to be thought of, imagined or dreamed up. Nothing can be made that is not first created in one mind or many minds, whether it be a car, computer, or can-opener. The same is true for your life. It is the things that you think about over and over which ultimately become the life you experience. In addition, the thoughts you think are filtered through beliefs you hold. Each belief acts like a filter, like wearing sunglasses. How many belief filters do you think you have? Do you have beliefs about money? Do you have beliefs about the current economic climate? Do you have beliefs about politics or social structure? What about the more mundane: do you have beliefs about parking spaces, litter, or stacking the dish washer in a certain way? When you get to thinking about it, you will come to recognise that you have beliefs about everything, from the biggest events to the everyday tasks. Depending upon how long you have been on the planet, the number of beliefs you have stored up will vary somewhat. It's true for all of us: the longer we've been alive, the more time we've had to acquire beliefs. Always remember, many of those beliefs are held in the subconscious mind.

The human brain is designed to think. According to Dr. Deepak Chopra, an average brain has around 75,000 thoughts per day, 60,000 of which are the same as yesterday's. With so many repetitive thoughts it is hardly surprising that we don't always find change easy to master. It is not simply that we have the thoughts, it is the nature of the thoughts and where they come from that present some of the greatest opportunities for learning and change.

How often have you woken up in the morning and felt like there is an entire committee meeting taking place in your head? It feels like there are at least ten of us in our minds, having a tug-of-war with our thoughts and all pulling in different directions. We are aware of these thoughts as they go around and around in our heads and sometimes it feels almost impossible to stop them. In addition to those that we are aware of, there are a huge amount that lay hidden in the subconscious mind. That's the part of the mind that we are unaware of, that lies hidden below the surface of consciousness. In the book 'Code to Joy' the authors explain that the ratio between conscious and subconscious thoughts is one to one million. Which means that for every single thing you know that you know, there are a million other things that you don't know you know. That's a lot of thoughts about a lot of things.

Between the conscious and subconscious minds there is a great deal going on, some of which is really useful. If you learned to drive a car a long time ago you probably no longer have to think about when to brake or when to use the accelerator, your subconscious has mastered that and you largely drive without thinking (not always such a good thing). On a deeper level, you don't have to constantly think about digesting your last meal or expelling unwanted carbon dioxide from your body as you breathe out.

At the same time, you have thoughts that may not be serving you, some you are aware of and some not. Our brains are constantly processing information from the moment we arrive on the planet in our little baby bodies. We don't have the conscious capacity to store everything we experience, so things get processed into the subconscious, out of sight, but not out of mind. At my live presentations I use Spot the spotless dog to assist me in demonstrating this point. Spot is a glove puppet (hand puppet) who thinks that he is the controller of his universe. What he doesn't see is it's my hand up his butt that's directing his life. We are very much like Spot, except that rather than a hand, it is our subconscious mind that is directing our lives. This brings a fresh understanding to the idea of having our heads up our butts, don't you think?

This concept may seem like a big leap if you haven't come across it before. If it is new to you, I invite you to stick with me and keep an open mind. This is actually far more straightforward than it might at first appear, and the principles and foundations you will discover through these pages are as ancient as life itself. They are also quite simple to apply. As you learn more about them you may find, just as I did, that something within you says, "Yes, I know this". Many people who discover these ideas have the same experience. It's almost like we have a deep inner knowing that has somehow been forgotten, a bit like having amnesia. So I invite you to keep reading, it gets better.

The programming is subtle

Perhaps, like me, you have spent some time in the yoyo land of diet - weight loss - no diet - weight gain - diet, etc. I *know* that eating a nutritious, balanced diet and taking regular exercise will keep my body healthy, and yet the call of fish and chips and peanut M&Ms still prompts me to make different choices. This is one, very simple, example of behaviour that can be driven by the hidden thoughts and beliefs in the subconscious mind. There could be many reasons for my erratic eating behaviour but I know that some of it is driven by subtle beliefs I have unconsciously adopted through conditioning and experience. As a child, how often were you rewarded with sweets (candy) or some other food treat for being well-behaved or achieving a great exam result? Do you still reward yourself that way?

When it comes to preparing the ground of our mind for the creation of new foundational practises, it is important to understand that most of the thoughts, words, feelings and actions up until this *infinite now* have been based on your survival instinct. You have learned to adapt to the life you were born into so that you could survive as long as possible. This is a good thing, even if it may have created some dysfunctional behaviour. Opening up to the idea that every thought we think is creating the experience of our life can lead people into what I call the 'guilt, blame, shame game'. It's the mind chatter that tells us how wrong or bad we are. Have you ever gone there?

It's that place in your mind where you give yourself a hard time because you feel guilty for something you did or didn't do. You feel miserable because you feel ashamed about what you did, didn't, should have, or could have done. Or you are angry and grumpy with 'them' because you *blame* them for something they did, didn't, should have, or could have done. Sometimes you may even find ways to blame others for your own perceived shortcomings. If you are like me, you have probably experienced this chatter voice at various times in your life. It is also known as the 'monkey mind' or the 'ego'. No matter where you are on the playing board for this game, it is an uncomfortable place to be. It is far better to remember that in every moment you have been doing the best you could to survive. Some times that 'best' will look plain ugly and sometimes it will look divinely radiant, either way, it is still the best you can do in each *infinite now* moment.

> *"We are not troubled by things, but by the*
> *opinions which we have of things."*
>
> ~ EPICTETUS

In my experience, our biggest difficulties in life aren't usually caused by the big events, or our actions, but rather by what we think and believe about the events and actions. Or put another way, by the meaning that we give to them, or make up about them.

Here's an example from my life: I was fortunate to be in a relationship which gifted me a live-in step daughter. I had parented other children earlier in my life, but had not previously lived with them. Having never had a baby of my own, I had not developed that essential parenting skill of selective hearing (if you have children, you know what I mean). I would hear every mutter my stepdaughter made under her breath, and the mutterings were not usually very polite. Sometimes, much to my chagrin, I would *react* rather than *respond* to her comments. My *reactions* would usually come at the end of a long day, when I was tired, grumpy and frustrated with a child who wouldn't comply with my requests or was trying to assert her own authority in her life. Conversely, at other times similar mutterings would have no effect, and I would simply hug her, tell her how much I loved her, and let the mutterings go without a passing thought. This almost always happened when I was feeling fresh, rested and happy about myself. In both of these scenarios I was doing the best I could, given the specific situation. It didn't excuse my behaviour and I frequently went back to her later and apologised. But now I have come to understand the nature of the mind, I can stay out of self-judgement and criticism and strive to do better next time. We'll talk about this more deeply later, but it's important to know that judgement and criticism *don't* facilitate lasting change, neither do they support a healthy self-image. I'm pleased to tell you that both my stepdaughter and I survived our time together and she is now one of my best friends.

Embracing the idea that our thoughts create our lives means taking complete responsibility for one's experience. This can be both daunting and liberating at the same time. I have met many people just learning about these concepts who are not always as compassionate with themselves or others as they could be. As you will learn, thinking differently and releasing old beliefs is a practise that gets easier with time.

When you start to look at your life a little more deeply and, perhaps, discover it's not quite where you want it to be, it's easy to fall into criticism and blame. At the start of a new personal journey I often hear things like: "I did a rubbish job if I created this all myself", or "what was in my consciousness to have created that?" As I have already pointed out, when we don't remember how powerful we are, the vast majority of our creation comes from the subconscious, the hidden stuff of our minds. There is no blame, guilt or shame to be considered. We are all always doing our best, and as Oprah says, "When we know better, we do better". The most important thing right now is to awaken your inner knowing and be gentle with yourself and have compassion for the journey you have taken thus far. Celebrate the fact that you are alive. Now you can start directing your powerful mind consciously into co-creating the life, career, health, relationships and money success that you desire.

Over my years of counselling, teaching and coaching people, I have discovered that almost all of us have a nagging voice in our head that keeps putting us down and telling us that we are somehow 'less than'. It's worth noting that we were not born with that voice, it is something we have learned on our journey. This 'inner critic', as it is often called, can be the destroyer of many great dreams. The problem, however, is not that we have that voice in our heads, it is that we believe it and we give it power over our actions. I'm all for taking the advice given in the title of Susan Jeffers book *Feel The Fear, And Do It Anyway*, or in this case, 'hear the voice that says you can't, and do it anyway.'

The great Zen teacher Cheri Huber reminds us, "That voice inside your head is not the voice of God, it just sounds like it thinks it is". We so easily get stuck in the hamster wheel of our thoughts and forget that they are only thoughts. In any moment we can change our thoughts, stop banging the drum of what was, and instead begin to write a new tune to accompany the life we would love to live.

When it comes to that voice inside our heads, there is another myth that it is well to throw out early in this book: The myth that self-criticism will enable behavioural change. Criticising yourself will not motivate you to change. If self-criticism and self-judgement worked as a motivator for change, we would all be living a life of bliss in a utopian world. Check in with yourself right now - how many years have you been consciously self-critical? How is it working for you and how has it moved you to change?

"Oh, but Juliet, you have to realise, if I stop criticising myself, then I'll just go completely off the rails." How many times have I heard this, or a variation of it? No, you won't go off the rails. It's quite simple, if you stop criticising yourself you will start to feel better about who you are and you will be more inclined to take gentle steps towards changing. It seems paradoxical, I know, but imagine you were teaching a child to ride a bicycle. You wouldn't (if you were in your right mind) shout, beat or otherwise abuse the child when they wobbled, or fell, or became fearful. Rather, you would cheer them on, coax them softly and help them back up when they fell, all the while telling them what a great job they were doing and how they will soon have cycle-riding mastered. That is what you would do, isn't it? If you would behave in such a supportive, loving way with a child, why would you behave any differently with yourself? It is time for you to become your own best friend and cheerleader. It is time to cherish your journey, develop some loving kindness towards yourself, and start to strengthen your own self-belief.

Just in case no one has ever told you before, here is the truth about you:

You are magnificent, you are beautiful, you are powerful, you are capable, you are brilliant and absolutely gorgeous. Your brain is just as powerful as everyone else's; you can achieve anything you want to. You are here, in your perfect, unique physical body suitcase to have fun, grow and thrive. Your presence on this planet is not some random accident, it is part of the fullness of Life. You are the place where the Infinite One becomes fully expressed in this finite world and you complete Creation. You are a radiant beacon of light and you are here to shine. If you weren't here, Life would be incomplete and the world a little dimmer.

This is true no matter what you have done or had done to you in your life. It doesn't matter if you can believe it about yourself or not, it is still true, and I hold that knowing for you until you awaken to it yourself.

When I share this in groups, people often come up to me at the end and say something like this, "You don't know me, if you knew what I'm really like and what my life is like, you would know that it's not true about me." If you are thinking this, I say to you what I say to them, "It is true about you, and I don't need to know you or anything about your life to know it is true because I know that there is only one thing in this life and everything is an expression of that one thing. Some people may call it God, but I call it Love. You are

Love expressing, even if you have forgotten, or have never known, and I am here to remember for you until you awaken".

I know that self-judgement and criticism are a problem for us all, so I created an e-course with five simple steps to help you breakthrough this learned habit. If you want some extra support on taming your inner critic, please go to my website (www.JulietVorster.com) and sign-up to receive the free e-course called *5 Steps to Freedom: Tame your critic and master your mind*.

Another tool to help you remember the truth of who you really are - a magnificent being of light with infinite potential here to have fun and grow - is to find a picture of yourself as a little baby. When we think of, or see, a young baby, it is so easy to recognise the innate perfection and wholeness that is before us. Perfect fingernails, eyelashes, tiny little ears and sparkling eyes. It is easy to see the potential and the miracle of creation when holding a baby. Find a picture of yourself, make some copies, and put them up around your home in places you will see them. As you look at the picture remember who you are and who you really came here to be before you learned who you had to be to get approval, acceptance and love. If you don't have any baby photos, don't worry, Google has thousands. Search through Google Images (or another search engine of your choice) until you find a cute-looking baby that you can believe you looked like. Then print out some copies and see yourself as that baby, with all the perfection and potential that we know to exist in a newborn. Remember there isn't a baby on this planet that doesn't love everything about themselves. Leave them without a nappy (that's a 'diaper' for my North American friends) for any length of time and they even love their poo. We have learned what we believe about ourselves and it's simply not true.

> *"A journey of a thousand miles starts with one step."*
>
> ~ LAO TZU

The purpose of this book is to inspire you to actually make changes in your life. The most effective way to bring forth these changes is to accept yourself right where you are, to let go of the judgement and criticism, and to start afresh on the level ground of self-compassion and an understanding of the power of your mind. It is from this place of awareness that we can step forward, trusting the principles of life, and honouring our own selves.

I look at my life as a series of experiments, each one building upon the last. It is from this ongoing experimentation that I have learned and adopted the following five foundational principles or practises that make up the first half of this book:

1. **Creative Thought: My thoughts create my reality so I practise staying conscious.**

   As I have already mentioned, everything that is created by people must first be thought up or imagined. It is said that necessity is the mother of invention. That holds true when it comes to creating your world with your thoughts. The things that we often think about, because of our need, get created. If we are lonely and want a new mate, then our constant attention on the idea of a new mate will create something. If most of the focus is on our loneliness and the absence of our dream partner, then we will create more absence and loneliness. If our attention is focussed on how we would love to be in a great relationship, celebrating the examples we see around us and filling our available time with fun things to do - regardless of our relationship status - then we are far more likely to manifest the partner of our dreams. Either way, our every thought is creating something in our physical world.

2. **Imagination: My imagination is the most creative part of my mind so I allow myself to dream big.**

You, like me, may have been told off as a child for daydreaming. I distinctly remember hearing my teacher say, "Wasting your time daydreaming won't get you anywhere in life. You have to work hard to get what you want." That's another myth that we'll get to later.

We now know that our imagination and the ability of our mind to create imagery is incredibly powerful in changing the material world. Our minds do not know the difference between something we remember, something we imagine (or invent), and something we are experiencing now. If we remember an incredibly funny moment, if we make one up in our imagination, or if we are experiencing it right now, our body chemistry and brain waves respond, regardless of the current 'reality' of the event.

It is time to become 'child-like', suspending the reality of *what is* and falling into the rich and fertile ground of our imaginations. It is here that anything is possible, and when we can conceive it and believe it, then we can achieve it.

3. **Feelings: The feelings I add to my thoughts provide jet fuel for my mental creations.**

Back in the sixties Neville Goddard wrote a book entitled *Feeling Is The Secret*. In this book, Goddard explains that the more we can tap into our feeling senses and incorporate them into our imaginings, the more powerful and speedy our creations are. The book also contains many letters from Neville's readers and students reporting their successes.

I have been practising this technique for many years in my own life and have discovered that adding emotional feelings and physical sensory experiences into my mental creations is like adding rocket fuel to a firework.

4. One Mind: My mind is one with the collective consciousness. I have a choice about where I place my mental attention, energy and focus.

We are all part of one collective mind. We are never separated from it, and no one is excluded. That's the good news, and the other news. On one hand we can tap into a universal intelligence even bigger than the internet. On the other hand, all those people who irritate us and believe the opposite to us, well, their mind is also part of the collective consciousness. This is where we get to practise keeping our attention on our own business and resist the urge to fall into other people's buckets.

I have often noticed how easy my life is when I stay in my own space with cats who don't talk back. I have said many times over that I never have PMS when I live on my own. Whilst this may be true, there is a limit to the amount of life we can experience when we are isolated (although spending time with cats can be a great inspiration). It is in our interactions with people that we are called forth to grow more and to become more, even when those people irritate us, don't want what we want, and believe different things than we do.

We are all here as part of the divine creation and each one of us is on our own personal journey to express that. The practice comes in focussing our attention on what we want to experience and not getting side-lined into everyone else's creation.

5. 3Ps: There are many ways to re-wire the mind. Practise, persistence and patience are required in any construction project, and I am always under construction.

When you get to know me, you will soon learn that one of my favourite words in the entire world is *practise*. I think our lives are one big practise where we keep running drills over and over until we get the play and we can move on to the next level, just like one of those annoying multilevel computer games. You must find all the gold, discover all the tools, defeat the 'baddies' and finally find the secret door to level up.

Some people play these games as though they were life itself, others take a very casual approach. Ultimately each one of us decides how seriously we take the game of life and how we choose to play. Regardless of our approach to playing the game, if we want to experience greater levels of thriving and success, there are some things it is beneficial to practise persistently. Then we get to practise being patient with the results.

The first half of this book will fully explore these ideas, and will also propose some additional concepts for your consideration. Each foundational concept builds on the previous one, and as you follow the steps and apply the practices, you will start to see changes in your life. In the second half of the book you will learn how to apply these concepts and principles in each of the five main areas of life: Health; Relationships; Vocation; Abundance and Spirituality.

Before concluding this opening chapter I wanted to remind you of the most basic principle: There is something intelligent that governs life. It causes the sun to rise and shine, it has all the planets in our solar system in perfect orbit, and it keeps us walking on the ground and not floating off in the ether. It is the same impelling force that transforms caterpillars into beautiful butterflies and prompts squirrels to bury their nuts. You are part of that intelligence. Never separate, always connected, no matter what. The biggest practise is in remembering, reconnecting and trusting. Oh yes, and you also need to keep breathing.

Even if the concepts you have read so far are new to you and you're not sure how to move forward, I invite you to open your heart and mind and be willing to experience something more. I have worked with hundreds of people from several countries over many years and I know how much these ideas can change our lives when we are willing to practise and apply them regularly to the daily experiences we have. Remember life is one great big practise and you are here to have fun and grow. Playing a game is always more fun when you get better at it. When you start to use the fullness of your amazing mind and become willing to step beyond your past experiences, you will develop the necessary skills to play the game of life like an Olympic athlete. When you reach this skill level it is amazing how fun practising can be.

Firm Foundations Are Essential

Chapter 2

I'LL BE SUCCESSFUL WHEN...

*"Success is liking yourself, liking what
you do, and liking how you do it."*

~ MAYA ANGELOU

Having picked up a book titled 'Igniting Success Beyond
Beliefs', I'm guessing you either want to experience greater success
in your life, or you are curious to know how beliefs affect your
success. The Maya Angelou quote above is one of over a hundred I
read when looking for a relevant opener for this chapter. That
research made me very aware that everyone has their own opinions
on success. I'm sure you have your opinions, but when did you last
spend some quality time considering what they are? Before we dive
deeper, here are some questions to ponder:

- What does success look and feel like to you?
- Do you think of yourself as successful?
- If not, what needs to change in your life so that you can
  embody success in a way that is meaningful to you?

Allow these questions to plant seeds in your mind. This isn't like
a school test; there are no right or wrong answers. No matter what
your current thoughts, opinions and beliefs are right now, it is my
intention to expand your mind with some new ideas. As you start to
think a little more deeply about your mind, your beliefs and the
world you live in, some new possibilities for success in your life will

be revealed.

So what is success anyway?

Some people may give success a financial figure: "I'll be successful when I make six figures or seven figures per year or per month". For others perhaps it is having their child go to university. For some, success may be defined by a social status, a particular car, or a certain type of house in a certain part of town. Or perhaps for you success is being able to feed yourself at the end of the day. Looking at success through the lens of modern life, it is clear to me that there is no single, perfect definition. When researching quotes I noticed that very few of the definitions referred to internal human experiences such as happiness or compassion. The vast majority were based on the achievement of external things, such as power or wealth.

You get to decide

The word 'success' didn't exist until sometime around 1530. It came from a Latin word meaning 'to come after', as a derivative of 'successor'. The modern definitions of success include 'completing one's goals' and 'the attainment of wealth, position, or honours'. Do any of those resonate with you? If not, continue contemplating how you define success in your life right now.

You may have been told what success means to others and those meanings may have been programmed into you in such a way that they have become your belief. There are many societal norms that are commonly accepted as signs of success, but what seems obvious to me from all this discussion is that **you** get to define success and what it means in your life. That may seem like a very radical idea, especially if you have been raised to conform to strict rules of living or to follow the family pattern of life. How you currently define success will depend greatly upon what you believe about yourself, about the world, and about your place within the world.

Let's take a moment to think about this. You are your own unique person. Who else could you possibly be? Every finger on your hand gives a unique print. The iris in each of your eyes is also unique. No other being exists on the planet that is like you. And that's the way it's designed. We are creatures naturally created to live in community, yet each one of us is our own perfectly unique being. So how can someone else's idea of success possibly be 100% true for you?

Without a clear personal definition of success, how do you know when you arrive? If you believe that success is something to strive for, and eventually achieve, then you probably want to create a road map of what it looks like and how to get there. Without knowing what success means to you, you will be constantly striving and moving forward without an end in sight. Such an approach could result in the creation of feelings of failure more than feelings of success. To discover a definition of success that is authentically yours, I invite you to do some investigation. First look at where your beliefs came from. Then evaluate how true they are for you today. After evaluation, you may want to apply some critical thinking to any discoveries, and review how the beliefs apply to the values you have in life. At the end of this chapter you will find an exercise to help you with this enquiry. For now I want to look a little deeper into how thoughts and beliefs change over time, and why this is relevant to our discussion about success and to the entire landscape of the book.

My definition of success has changed many times through my life and I'm sure yours has too. As a younger person, without realising it, I automatically wore many of my parents' beliefs like a coat. These beliefs included an unspoken definition of success. If I were to capture that definition it would look something like this:

✓ Success is completing a university degree, getting a good, stable, job with a lasting future, one that pays enough for you to buy your own home and live in a good area.

✓ Success is getting married to someone of the same social and economic background as you, having two children and at least one cat.

✓ Success is taking a family holiday in the summer and driving a reasonably new car that is always kept clean and tidy.

✓ Success is having a well-organised, clean and tidy home, not too cluttered, that closely resembles a show home.

✓ Success is keeping yourself to yourself, staying out of other people's business, and meeting for coffee once a week with a girlfriend.

If I were to actually apply this definition of success to my life, I would have failed on everything except the cat. If I believed that not conforming to this definition means I am a 'failure', I could easily find myself feeling bad or sad, but the truth is it's simply not my definition of success. Ironically, it is only as I write this that I see clearly how much of my early struggle came from my not fitting into someone else's unspoken and subtle but nevertheless very present definition of success. Could this be true for you too? Take a moment to think about any hidden, subtle definitions of success that may still be at work within you.

When we think about how success is defined in the developed countries of the world it is all based on external things. This would be an okay plan if people felt good about themselves when they 'achieved success', but on the whole they are miserable. What if the world has got its idea of success all back to front? What if we are defining success in the wrong way, and looking for success in the wrong place? What if success comes from the inside out and has nothing to do with what the Tao Te Ching calls "the world of the 10,000 things"? It's not that achieving external results, or driving a sexy sports car, are bad things. But they come and go throughout our life. Defining our success by transient external things is unlikely to create the deep and lasting sense of inner wellbeing that most of us are seeking.

To look at this from a different perspective, let's talk about the dynamic relationship between your thoughts, your feelings and your body. In the moments we glimpse success, physical sensations are generated in the body. Butterflies in the stomach, an increased heart rate, rapid breathing and even a skin flush are all physical expressions we may notice when success strikes. When we experience success we'll often punch the air or jump up and down. This clearly demonstrates that success is more than just an achievement in the world. It is a very intimate visceral experience.

How do you know?

> *"Ever since Happiness heard your name It has been running through the streets trying to find you."*
>
> ~ HAFIZ

Just for a moment I invite you to float down a new river of thought with me to consider the connection between our external experiences, our thoughts, our beliefs, and our emotions. Which comes first, and how do you know?

One of the things I teach is the concept that our thoughts and beliefs create our life. Quantum science tells us that everything is driven by consciousness, and yet when it comes to the organism known as the human body, there are some interesting things that happen.

- There is a great TED talk (if you don't know TED talks, you can Google them) with Amy Cuddy, a Harvard social psychologist, who has researched the effect our body posture has on our hormones and therefore our psychology. She discovered that if we stand in certain 'power poses' for a period of two minutes (my favourite is the Wonder Woman pose), the chemistry in our body changes. The 'I feel powerful' hormones increase and the 'I am an unworthy worm' hormones decrease. The net result of this is that we feel more confident. This research indicates that changes in our experience do not only come from changing our thoughts on the inside, but by making changes with our body on the outside.

- With modern technology, science is better able to scan the brain without having to cut open the skull and stick electrodes into the actual brain (definitely a great improvement for any volunteers). Research has shown that movement impulses take place in a body part, such as a finger, before the brain signal has fired to tell the finger to move. That's kind of spooky. Your body can move without your brain telling it to.

- Recent research has discovered that the correct balance of good bacteria in the gut can affect our state of mind. Taking good quality probiotics and balancing the bacteria through our digestive system has been shown to improve symptoms of depression, OCD, ADHD and other mental health diagnoses.

Now, having read these short pieces of information, when it comes to feeling and thinking, which comes first in your body? Do you feel a certain feeling or sensation and then think a relevant thought? Or is it the other way around? Does thinking a particular thought take you to experiencing a related kind of feeling? If you're not really sure, then you are in total alignment with science. Despite many research hours having been poured into this enquiry there are no conclusive results yet.

No matter whether feeling or thinking come first, the two go together because we are not just our mind, we are an entire, very complex, many trillion celled organism called a human being. Quantum science tells us that every cell has consciousness, has its' own life purpose, and is operating in co-operation with all the other cells in its neighbourhood. No single part of your experience is separate from any other. It is valuable to open your mind to this understanding because the co-dependencies and interdependencies that happen within your body all come together to help you grow and thrive. Think of your body like a great ants' nest or termite mound - each cell is like an individual ant or termite, with its own particular job and its own way of interacting with other members of the colony. It is only when each individual comes together and operates in harmony with the others that everything runs perfectly.

Your beliefs direct your thoughts

In truth, although our thoughts and feelings are incredibly powerful and they are constantly creative, sitting behind our thoughts are our beliefs. It is the beliefs we hold about things that really impact the direction of our experience. What you currently believe about success is determining what you, and your physical body, are experiencing in a very real way. Your beliefs about success could be affecting your mood, your mental clarity, your relationships, your financial prosperity, and even the way you achieve results in everyday life. The effect of your beliefs can be negative, positive or neutral.

How you perceive success is affecting your everyday life experience to a greater or lesser degree. What if you could directly change your experience for the better by changing your definition of success and the beliefs you hold about that definition?

Are you opting in?

> *"There are two primary choices in life: to accept conditions as they exist, or accept the responsibility for changing them."*
> ~ DENIS WAITLEY

Society in the West puts a huge amount of emphasis on 'success'. We test our children to within an inch of their lives to see if they are succeeding academically. We have all sorts of polls and metrics in our communities and businesses to measure success. Then there are the media, who seem to have their entire focus on comparing levels of success: the top earners; the most beautiful people; the biggest houses; the best actors etc. This all adds up to huge cultural pressure to somehow conform to an unachievable 'success' target.

> *"The only sin is compara-sin."*
> ~ JIM TURRELL

When we compare ourselves and our success with anyone else's, we are setting ourselves up to fail. Imagine comparing a lemon and a banana. On the surface they are both a shade of yellow, does that make them the same? How successful would it be if you made up a recipe using a banana where it called for a lemon? You might be disappointed with the results. Comparing ourselves, in any way, with others is no different to comparing a banana and a lemon. Surface similarities do not mean that the two are identical in any way. Comparing ourselves and our experience of success can lead to all kinds of challenges and dysfunctional behaviours. When it comes to success there is only one useful measurement - "What does success mean to me?" Let's find out. What *does* it mean to you?

How often have you actually sat down and thought about what *success* means to you? Not what it means to your parents, partner or boss, but how you define it and how that definition affects your life and the way you live it. I keep asking these same questions because I hope that your ideas of success are already evolving. If they are not, at the very least I am planting a seed for the future that may germinate at the perfect moment in your life.

Take a breath and close your eyes. Allow any new awareness concerning success to come to mind. Don't judge what comes up, this is about you becoming more aware of your thoughts and beliefs, you are on the first step of getting to know yourself better, so be gentle with yourself. When you have some sense of what you think and feel about success open your eyes, take a breath, and be here now.

Remember, this book is an invitation to play full out and actually make some changes in your life so that you can ignite success beyond beliefs - whatever that might be for you. The only way to do that, is to put your play suit on and do the exercises.

Foundations for living

"It is not the beauty of a building you should look at; it's the construction of the foundation that will stand the test of time."

~ DAVID ALLAN COE

I believe we have five key areas that all need to be nourished and kept in balance and harmony with each other:

- Body / Health
- Relationships
- Career / Vocation
- Prosperity / Abundance
- Spirituality

These areas are like the five main rooms in a house - the sitting room, dining room, kitchen, bedroom and bathroom. For now you get to decide which room represents which area in your life. It is difficult to imagine a house without these rooms, or at least areas within rooms dedicated to the different functions. I know people who live in a great big open plan space, one room with different areas. Whichever it is for you, we all need to relax, be in community, prepare food, eat, bathe and rest.

In addition to these five areas, I have already set out five foundational principles for how to live a thriving life and achieve success beyond beliefs, in the previous chapter. Let me remind you of those:

1. Creative Thought
2. Imagination
3. Feelings
4. One Mind
5. 3Ps

Imagine coming upon a building site, looking down onto the foundations and seeing five square blocks, each one a different size and height. How stable and level would a building be that was built on these foundational blocks? When we think of foundations in a building we have a general understanding that they need to be level, equally sized, strong and supportive in order for the building to be stable and viable. Why would building a foundation for our lives be any different? As humanity has evolved, we have grown through IQ (Intelligence Quotient - the ability to measure and evaluate academic intelligence) to EQ (Emotional Quotient - the ability to measure and evaluate emotional intelligence) and now we are moving into SQ (Spiritual Quotient - the ability to measure and evaluate spiritual intelligence). These evolutions make it all the more important to establish meaningful and supportive foundations in our lives. Humanity is moving up in consciousness. We are moving beyond wanting our basic needs to be met and into the realm of finding meaning and purpose to our lives. To stay in this higher realm of consciousness it is valuable to have confidence that our foundations will continue to support all our basic needs and allow this upward spiral to continue.

Cindy Wigglesworth, author of the book *"SQ21: The 21 Skills of Spiritual Intelligence"*, says this, "I define Spiritual Intelligence as 'the ability to behave with Compassion and Wisdom while maintaining inner and outer peace (equanimity), regardless of the circumstances'."

Which brings us back around to the idea of success and how you define it. When you read Cindy's definition, do you think you would feel successful if *you* could maintain inner and outer peace, no matter what was happening around you? I know I would. Like me, you probably manage it sometimes, but wouldn't it be great to be living from that place of spiritual intelligence all the time?

Climbing the ladder

Humans are the only animals on the planet that collect things that are not directly required for their survival. We then compare the things we have collected with the things others have collected, and use that comparison to judge and measure our 'success'. However, what we are doing internally is judging and measuring our personal worth and value. We are using the 'stuff' that we have collected, or the absence of it, to give our lives meaning and establish a reference point for who we think we are in the world.

- How's that working for you? Do you think there could be a different way?
- What *if* you were fundamentally 'successful' from the moment of your arrival on the planet?
- What *if* there was a natural understanding of success and how to achieve it within you, but you've forgotten?
- What *if* success is something that isn't dependent on 'stuff', academic achievement, your (or your family's) social or economic status, or any other worldly measure?
- What *if* success is your birthright and is something that can never be measured, compared or removed?

- What *if* success comes from the inside out?

Take a breath and re-read these questions. Take a moment to be with them. Allow their content to wash over you as you contemplate your answers.

You were born perfectly successful. No matter how healthy or otherwise your physical body or mind is. Regardless of your parents' desire to have you and keep you, or not. Irrespective of your perceived beauty or cuteness. You are successful because success is your birthright, it isn't something that is earned or dependent on anything external. And although you can forget and disconnect from it, your innate success cannot be taken away. You are made of the infinite energy of life. Although you are your own unique person, the intelligent energy that created you and from which every atom of your body is made is absolutely perfect, and so are you.

That doesn't mean you will automatically feel or see yourself as successful right now. I fully understand that you may be reading this, looking around at your current life circumstances, and thinking, "She's talking utter nonsense". I well recall times in my life when I would have been thinking exactly the same. I have come on a long journey from believing I am totally unloveable and worthless. And I know that if I can do it, anyone can. Any challenges you may be experiencing in life are not the truth of you. If there is only one intelligent energy in this universe and we are all created from it, then it must be true that you are that same energy. You are created from the wholeness of life and you are always connected to the infinite intelligence of creation.

Think of it this way: Imagine looking out upon nature; the trees, grass, shrubs, plants and flowers. As you look at all the different elements of nature, do you think one thing is more successful than any other? It may be that some are more prolific. Some are bigger, some smaller. But there is an eternal flow of growth, change and decay to be observed, where no one thing is more successful than any other. It is the symbiotic relationship of all the elements that creates a thriving collaborative eco-system. That's a great model for us humans to follow. When we step away from the external idea of success and the natural state of competition it creates, we can reclaim our equanimity and step into thriving.

It is time to claim your own innate magnificence. Believing anything less about yourself is based on experiences and things you learned that were not true. By the end of this book you will be stepping out beyond those beliefs and igniting greater levels of success in ways that are not subject to the whims of fashion or public opinion.

I feel successful almost all the time because I choose, very actively, to master my mind and my body. There are those moments, when my fearful self stages a takeover of my body's control centre, when I forget who I really am, and fall back into playing what I call the 'guilt, blame, shame game'. What I know about that is the more I practise what I teach in my own life, the easier it becomes to reclaim the control centre and get back to success, joy, peace, gratitude and love. And trust me, some days it really is a practice. You know the feeling when you have to drag yourself out of bed to go to the gym and you really don't want to go, even though you know you'll feel great when you finish? Just like that, sometimes it's a practice.

This may be a quantum leap of an idea for you, and you may have all kinds of evidence that says it's a silly idea. That's okay. I simply invite you to park any disbelief for now and allow the possibility of this idea to start bubbling around your mind. We'll come back to it later.

The one thing I would love for you to take away from this chapter is that when it comes to success, it's an inside job. *You* get to decide what it means and how you measure it. And, it's okay for you to change your mind.

Awareness Exercise - at the end of each chapter you will find an exercise designed to help you get to know yourself better and increase your awareness of the things you think and believe. If you are serious about Igniting Success Beyond Beliefs, I encourage you most sincerely to take the time to do the exercises as you read the book.

Chapter 2 Awareness Exercise - I'll be successful when...

I invite you to take some time with your journal and write at the top of the page:

"I'll be successful when . . . "

Then start to complete that sentence by writing down as many different answers as you can. You may want to leave the list open, so when inspiration strikes you can add new answers to it. This is an *awareness exercise*, there is no right or wrong, no good or bad. It is simply an opportunity to discover something about what you believe about success.

Now take a look at the answers you have put down. When you read that list, do you truly feel they are things *you* believe? Or perhaps they are things that you have absorbed from - or been programmed with - by your family, religion, school, or society at large. Again, it is really important to remember that there is no right or wrong. It's all about awareness and beginning to understand your thoughts and beliefs at a deeper, more conscious level.

As I mentioned earlier, I believe we have five key areas that all need to be nourished and kept in balance and harmony with each other: Body/Health; Relationships; Career/Vocation; Prosperity/Abundance; Spirituality. Take a moment to review the answers you wrote. Can you recognise them as relating to these five areas of your life? Perhaps you have lots of things in one or two areas and very few or even none in other areas. It's perfectly okay to be right where you are. As you read this book, and play with the exercises and experiments, it is my intention that your attitude to the entire concept of success will alter and your mind will open to greater possibilities for your life.

Now that you have some awareness of success and its definition in your life, let's look at how success feels. Look at each item on your list and read it aloud.

- As you speak it out, how does it feel in your body?
- Where do you experience the feeling?
- Does it make you feel light and free or heavy and restricted?
- Is there a connection between the definitions that feel authentic and the lighter feeling?

Just notice. You don't have to make up any stories about what that means, this is just an opportunity for greater awareness. Remember to breathe. Often as we start a deeper level of personal enquiry we forget to breathe as we become engrossed with trying to figure things out. I have made one significant discovery in life - breathing is essential. Try giving it up and I'm sure you'll agree.

You have now added a surprising amount of data about success, what it means to you, and how you feel about it. It is remarkable how much information we have within us that we don't commonly seek to connect with. Isn't it amazing that a few simple questions can bring forth so many different answers?

You may find that you have no current definitions of success that make you feel good. That's okay. Do your best to stay in the present moment and remember that this is just an awareness of where you are in this infinite now. You are always evolving and expanding, always moving into the *greatest yet to be* of your life, and your history does not predict your destiny.

Alternatively, you may have very few definitions that make you feel restricted or heavy, which is also perfectly okay. I am a great believer that we are always in the perfect place, at the perfect time, having the perfect experience. Even if it doesn't look very pretty or feel very joyous, it is bringing us the perfect opportunity for our growth and learning.

Chapter 3

YOU'LL SEE IT WHEN
YOU BELIEVE IT

*"It's not the events of our lives that
shape us, but our beliefs as to
what those events mean."*

~ TONY ROBBINS

When looking for a title for this chapter I chose this book title from Wayne Dyer very deliberately. "You'll See It When You Believe It" was the first book I read by Dr. Dyer and it was one of the first times I really started to think about what I believe, and how it was that I took on those beliefs in the first place. I came to realise that, directly or indirectly, I learned them. I was taught by the environment in which I grew up. By my parents, school teachers, friends, ministers, extended family and by society at large, I was taught what was an acceptable belief system in my environment. And so were you.

This idea brings to mind the song 'You've got to be carefully taught' from the musical South Pacific. The song speaks about having to be taught the things that your parents think, and taught to do the things that are socially acceptable in your parents' community. If you don't know the song, you could look it up on YouTube and listen to the lyrics. In today's Western society the lyrics are controversial, but the message contained within, that we learn what our parents and their social set believe, is still very true today.

What do you believe?

We, as humans, act out and behave in the way we do because of the beliefs we hold about ourselves, life, other people and the world at large. We have beliefs about everything. Some are very strong, some are like passing clouds, but most we are unaware of. Whichever category they fall into, they all impact our life in some way. Having beliefs about everything totals up to a huge amount, but where do they come from and where do they reside?

Just for a moment close your eyes and think about cats; now ask yourself, "When it comes to cats, I believe…"

Immediately you will have a wide range of thoughts. Depending on what you think about cats, those thoughts may be positive or negative but they are not right or wrong, true or false, they are simply what you believe about cats.

As a confirmed 'mad cat woman', I believe cats are lovely and that a house becomes a home when it has a cat in it. I recognise that this statement is not fundamentally right or wrong, it's just what I believe.

Where did that belief come from? In my case I was raised in a cat-loving home, where both my parents adored cats and we were never long without one. Perhaps you are nodding along with this, because your experience was similar to mine, or perhaps you are shaking your head vigorously because you don't like or understand cats and were raised in a dog-loving house or have never had a pet and really don't get what all the fuss is about. Regardless of where you are in the 'cat' conversation, hopefully you can see that your beliefs on the subject are just that, beliefs. They were formed somewhere along the river of your life and they influence your behaviour around cats.

Take a moment to breathe into this concept of belief and then take an objective look at your cat beliefs. Are they facts? Your immediate reaction to that may be a resounding "Yes!" But think again, can you categorically prove what you believe is true, in every case, all the time? Perhaps there are some elements of fact, but more likely, most is opinion based on belief. And the seeds of those beliefs may well have been planted very early.

Having been raised in a cat-friendly home, it is very unlikely that I would have gained negative beliefs about cats. I could have gained negative beliefs about dogs if both my parents had been afraid of dogs. Fortunately for me, that was not the case, but it could have been.

Cats and dogs are a simple, yet often divisive, example of belief. Just for a moment think about an average day in your life. With this new perspective on beliefs, how much do you think your actions, reactions, words and behaviour are driven by your beliefs?

Take a breath for a moment; what do you think about obesity or body image in the media? What do you think about rich people, intelligent people, beggars or addicts? Do you have strongly held beliefs about some or all of these subjects or do they not really interest you? My beloved can become animated about parking spaces and tax forms. Perhaps you have other favourite subjects on which you hold strong opinions. Regardless of where your strong beliefs lie, just for now have a think about where they came from. Did someone directly tell you what to believe? Did you learn from watching and listening to others as they expressed their beliefs? Or did they get synthesised through your experiences over a long period of time? As you think about where they came from and how they come to be in your mind, being really objective, are they true?

> *"All our words are but crumbs that fall down from the feast of the mind."*
>
> ~ KHALIL GIBRAN

Beliefs act upon every element of life. When it comes to the words we use, and the meaning we give to those words, our beliefs make a huge difference. At their most basic, words are a bunch of syllables strung together. In a particular language, or country, we humans have made an agreement about what each word means or represents. Those basic meanings have then been recorded in something we have agreed to call a dictionary. Specific words in a common language can have totally different meanings depending on the country they are used in, and by the age group of the people using them. Here are a couple of examples:

> In the US the word 'fanny', as in 'fanny pack', refers generally to the bottom. In the UK a 'fanny' is a slang term for vagina and 'fanny pack' translates to 'bum-bag', which has an entirely different meaning again in the US.

> When I was at school, the word 'wicked' meant things like 'evil, bad, corrupt', and older people still use it in that way. To the younger generation 'wicked' means something that is really good.

Language is always in a state of flux, just like humanity - it is always evolving and changing. When we collectively agree upon a certain meaning for a certain word it has no feeling or energy attached to it. However, once we start to use words in everyday life, how we use them and the tone we add to our speech adds an energetic charge. This energy tends to generate a fresh meaning which we then wrap in our beliefs. As soon as we have added our beliefs to words we have created something new which can be used as a weapon, against ourselves and others.

WORDS   WORDS   WORDS

WORDS   WORDS   WORDS

WORDS WORDS WORDS

WORDSWORDSWORDS
WORD**SWORDS**WORDS

A good example of a word that has become a sword is the word 'god'. A tiny little word. Yet look at all the belief that is poured into those three letters. What feelings and beliefs come up in you when you read 'God'? Are you thinking I have a typo because I didn't use a capital 'g' on the first reference? A quick check in Google tells me there are somewhere between 250,000 and 600,000 words in the English language, and that's only one language. For many of those words you won't have a strong belief, but for many others, you will. It's valuable to think about this. You may have beliefs and emotional charges wrapped up in words that aren't directly connected to their dictionary meaning. This could cause you to have a disproportionate reaction to a word or phrase someone uses in all innocence. Two other words that carry a vast range of different beliefs are 'money' and 'love'. I'm sure you can think of some from your life that hold strong belief and feeling for you. Remember, beliefs are not wrong or right, they are understandings and interpretations we synthesise through our experiences and thoughts. At any moment we can re-evaluate them and let them go if they are causing us pain and suffering.

Our beliefs are a synthesis of our experiences.

Just looking back to chapter two I can see that the definition of success I *perceived* from my childhood is one based on the filters that I acquired as I grew up in my home environment. They were never directly laid out or spoken; I made them up based on my mental and emotional interpretation of my environment and experiences. It is perfectly possible that if my parents read that list they would be baffled by how I came up with it. It's time to think a little deeper about what we believe.

A very large percentage and quite probably all of your behaviour is at least *influenced* by what you believe. Each belief acts like a filter or a pair of sunglasses. It gives you a slightly different view of the world compared to your neighbour's. That view is your view, just like the cats and dogs example, it's not right or wrong, good or bad, it's just your view, gained through the lens of your life experience.

So if our beliefs are neither good nor bad, why do they sometimes cause so much trouble? In my life I usually experience drama, hurt or upset when I have decided that my beliefs are *facts* and they are *right*. When I take the position that I am right, by definition I am automatically making someone else *wrong*. That is how wars get started. Thinking our filters are *correct facts* and that people with different filters are wrong, bad, stupid, ignorant or lacking in some basic level of humanity is a recipe for disaster, whether it's on a personal or national level. We often see this demonstrated in religion and politics but the same challenge demonstrates in many different ways every day of our lives.

The Oxford dictionary says that a belief is "an acceptance that something exists or is true, especially one *without proof*'. The interesting thing about this definition is that we often think we do have proof because we haven't evaluated our beliefs; instead we have held them firm and treated them like facts.

Here's an example that I often use when I teach:

> *There was once a young boy called Joe, when he was five years old it was time for him to go out into the world and start school. Joe's mother was a very sensible woman who loved her son very much, and so on the way to school on the very first day, she said to Joe, "Joe, you are getting to be a big boy now, you will be meeting all kinds of people, but you must never talk to strangers. Do you*

understand? Never talk to strangers. Some grown-ups are not kind, so if you don't know the person, don't talk to them."

This is great advice for young Joe who is a sensitive young man and takes this cautious instruction into his five-year-old mind as a belief that says, "grown ups I don't know are not safe and I must never talk to them."

When Joe gets to school he is introduced to his teacher and joins his class. He always participates well in class and very much enjoys school. He is outgoing and popular with the other children. One day a different teacher comes to teach them, one that Joe hasn't been introduced to. He immediately becomes nervous and shy. He stops participating and sharing and has a strange, nervous feeling in his tummy. In a few days, his regular teacher comes back and everything returns to normal in Joe's young life.

Joe's mother regularly reminds him not to speak to strangers, and adds to the story that some people are bad and want to hurt children. Every time he hears this instruction, his belief that unknown adults are a great threat to him grows.

Each time Joe comes across a 'stranger', even if it's in what may be considered a safe environment, he closes down and stops speaking. This pattern repeats itself regularly as Joe progresses through school, but as each teacher spends time with Joe, they only see 'their Joe', either the confident, engaged Joe or the shy, withdrawn Joe. No one really notices throughout Joe's school career that he is great with some adults and won't say a word to others.

In Joe's mind the belief that was programmed at five years old has never been reprogrammed and, as he continues to grow, he operates with that filter in his mind, even though he has long forgotten the instruction on a conscious level. When he finally steps out into the world he is a quiet, withdrawn young man, very disassociated from others and with almost no ability to make friends.

This story demonstrates the power of our minds to receive a piece of information, translate it, give it our own interpretation and meaning, and then add it to our internal operating system and use it to run our lives. This is one way beliefs are formed, and the more beliefs we develop, the more filters we have in place and the more our new pieces of information are affected by the existing beliefs or filters. No wonder our minds sometimes feel really full up.

> *"The way we talk to our children*
> *becomes their inner voice."*
>
> ~ PEGGY O'MARA

In our story Joe interpreted a very specific verbal instruction and made it part of his personal belief system. Another way in which beliefs are formed is by what I call 'organic osmosis'. Our powerful minds are constantly collecting subtle data about our environment, the people in it, and the way those things feel. We collect that data through our standard five senses and through our inner knowing, intuition or gut feeling. This is great and not so great all at the same time. When we absorb all this information as adults we have our rational, objective, conscious mind that can generally filter and add context to situations and events. Children, particularly those age seven and under, don't have that level of objectivity. If you have ever spent time with young children you will know that they don't understand sarcasm or subtle humour because at that age the mind accepts everything it hears as fact. Because the conscious mind is not yet fully developed, young children don't understand context. This could lead them to completely misunderstand something they overhear in an adult conversation. That misunderstanding may create a false belief that gets stored in the subconscious mind without anyone ever noticing.

When a child lives in an environment where parents are constantly arguing, the child is absorbing subtle beliefs about relationships: the role of men and women, how to express emotions, and myriad other pieces of information that are automatically processed into beliefs. These are then packed into the subconscious mind without any conscious awareness. Add into that argumentative environment a particular subject matter such as money, addictions, parenting differences, and/or extreme anger, and the child creates even more beliefs that we have no idea are forming. Years later, as adults, we then wonder why we have money trouble or difficulty expressing emotions or one of the many other challenges we experience in everyday life.

Take a breath and allow your mind to drift back into some of the memories you have from the first seven years of your life. What beliefs might have been formed by your young mind in those situations? Whether they are happy memories or otherwise, take a moment to imagine the kinds of beliefs that may have been created.

"Give me a child until he is seven and I will give you the man", is a saying attributed to the Jesuits. It speaks well to the developmental growth that happens in a young mind. I have heard it said that by the age of seven, sometimes referred to as the 'age of reason', a child has formed a complete set of basic beliefs about life and how it will support them. From that point forward those beliefs play out in the subconscious mind and create subtle situations which bring forth more 'evidence' to prove that the already held beliefs are true.

I can certainly see how that has been true in my life, does it resonate with you? Have you ever found yourself in what appears to be a repeat of a similar situation, except that the people involved have changed? For example, you don't get on with your boss because he/she is micro-managing you, so you change jobs, only to find yourself with a new boss who behaves just the same. Or you leave a partner because they don't clean up after themselves in the bathroom, you get into a new relationship, and six months later you are out the door, fed-up with another dirty bathroom. By the way, you now know I don't like being micro-managed or dirty bathrooms. I try to use as many of my own experiences as I can when illustrating these ideas because I continue to learn and practise every day in my own life. I am no different from you, I may have been studying these ideas a bit longer, but I still put my trousers on one leg at a time, just like you do.

The Flea and the Elephant

"In measuring the activity of the subconscious mind as compared to the conscious mind, we're looking at a factor of about a million to one."
~ FROM 'CODE TO JOY' BY GEORGE PRATT & PETER LAMBROU

The subconscious (or unconscious) mind is something that science still knows relatively little about and yet we know it contains a huge amount of data, information and beliefs. Remember that in chapter one I told you about the book 'Code to Joy', which tells us that the modern understanding of the mind reflects a one to one-million ratio between the conscious and subconscious. That means that for every one thing you know you know, your amazing mind is handling another one million things at the same time. The authors of 'Code To Joy' use a wonderful story all about a flea who thinks he's king of the world, and his pet elephant, to illustrate this ratio. I have found that story to be one of the best illustrations to help me understand how our subconscious mind impacts our daily lives. This research goes to prove that no matter what beliefs you may have installed about how intelligent or otherwise you are, your brain is an organic super-computer. Smile, now you have evidence that you are not dumb or lacking intelligence, your brain is busy with millions of bits of information every second.

As we journey together, please remember that a huge amount of what is happening in your mind is in that hidden portion of the mind (which is more than just your brain) that we call the subconscious. I personally prefer the word 'subconscious' rather than 'unconscious', although the words can be used equally well to describe that part of the mind. I prefer subconscious because 'sub' speaks to me about that part of the mind which is hidden below the surface. That means it is accessible, and when we start to scratch the surface, we can begin to uncover some of the things that appear hidden. You could think of it as an excavation project a bit like they do on an ancient site. Uncovering years of dust and dirt.

This book is designed to help you to uncover these hidden false beliefs and to set your mind free from a subconscious operating system that may be keeping you from your greatest joy and from living the life that you are born to live.

I have been studying this field very actively since 2001, and as my own guinea pig, I have plenty of evidence to show that as I do my inner work, spend time discovering hidden false beliefs, and then practise certain things to change my mental program, I can change how my life looks on the outside. These external changes are wonderful and yet for me the most important thing has been that I have changed how I feel on the inside. I now live 95% of my life with a deep sense of inner peace and calm, I have purpose, I am very comfortable with who I am and I feel fulfilled in every way. My aim is to give you the tools so that you can take your own action and achieve this for yourself.

That other 5% proves that I'm still human and that even after so many years of practise and self-discovery, I occasionally get thrown off balance by life's events. It is not that life changes when we grow our awareness, life still happens in just the same way for me as it does for you. The difference is I no longer believe all the thoughts I think.

Chapter 3 Awareness Exercise - So what do you really believe?

This exercise is designed to help you discover some of those hidden false beliefs. It is really important to be gentle with yourself when you do this exercise and remember that there is no right or wrong, no good or bad. This is an opportunity for you to come to know *you* a little better and to start down the road of igniting success beyond beliefs.

Before you get started with the first part of this exercise you may want to read through it a couple of times or record it into your phone or computer so that you can listen to it as you take the journey.

Close your eyes and take a breath, then take another breath, this time a little deeper, and now another, deeper still. Keeping your eyes closed, imagine gazing into a deep lake - the water is clear and the surface is still. You can see down into the water a very long way. Hold that vision and take some more deep breaths. When you feel ready, open your eyes and begin the exercise.

Take a fresh piece of paper or a new page in your journal and at the top write:

'I believe I am the kind of person who is...'

Now complete that sentence in as many different ways as you can. The deeper you are willing to go the more discoveries you will make. Try to go beyond what you think you know and allow yourself to access the subconscious; you may be surprised by what comes up.

Once you have some answers to that question, continue to do exactly the same with each of these following questions:

'I believe I am the kind of person who isn't...'

'I believe I am the kind of person who can't...'

'I believe I am the kind of person who can...'

Remember to be gentle with yourself, allow any emotions that come up to be okay with you, don't judge them or get stuck in any of the stories that come up. Breathe into the answers and allow a sense of excitement to bubble up as you start to uncover some hidden treasure that will enable you to free yourself from the clutter of your mind and move you further towards your greatest yet to be.

You may have discovered some challenging thoughts and beliefs. Even these are treasures, although they are sometimes a little more difficult to unwrap. As you continue through the book you will learn new tools to help you process and re-order your discoveries. If you find yourself feeling unsettled you may consider connecting with a professional consultant or therapist to help you process your discoveries.

You'll See It When You Believe It

66

Chapter 4

GOING BEYOND POSITIVE THINKING

"Whether you think you can or
think you can't, you're right."

~ HENRY FORD

Foundation 1
Creative Thought: My thoughts create my
reality so I practise staying conscious.

Dr. Joe Dispenza, whose website describes him as a Neuroscientist, Chiropractor, Lecturer and Author, says in the movie 'What The Bleep Do We Know', that our brains process 400 billion bits of information every second, but we are only aware of 2,000 of those. That's every brain, not just the really clever people; that's you and me.

I can't really get my head around '400 billion' bits of anything, but I know it's a lot. How would your life be different if you could learn to use even a small amount of that brain power in a directed way so that you become happier, healthier, less stressed, have more time, more money and better relationships?

Before you allow your mind, which is currently thinking, "Yeah, right, like that's even possible", to persuade you to put this book down, I invite you to once again read the opening quote.

In Christian scripture it says, "According to your faith let it be done to you". Ernest Holmes translated that sentence into "It is done unto you as you believe". The ancient Huna tradition, from Hawaii says, "The world is what you think it is". The Buddha said this: "Whatever a monk keeps pursuing with his thinking and pondering, that becomes the inclination of his awareness". There are many references throughout history telling us what these few words from Henry Ford declare so clearly. Whatever you believe is true for you. Having read the earlier chapters, are you starting to wonder a bit more about what you do believe and how that may be affecting your life?

As we start to learn more about our beliefs, the brain, and how everything works to create our lives, it's useful to take a quick look at the idea of 'positive thinking' and to let go of some ideas that do not serve us.

When you read the term 'positive thinking' you may have one or many of the following thoughts: it's good, it's bad, it's new age nonsense, it's not for me, it's the cornerstone of my life, I can't do it, it's just thinking happy thoughts, it's easy to stay positive - and on we go. There has been so much written about this concept in my life time and yet it may still be possible that you have never even come across the term 'positive thinking'.

No matter what you may have heard, read, or believe about positive thinking, I aim to expand your mind with some new ideas. I will then lead you into a fresh understanding of how your mind works, in collaboration with your entire body system - finally explaining how your powerful, amazing, brilliant mind can be used to create an entirely different life experience.

Choices, choices, choices

In each and every moment of your life you are making choices.

Some are totally beyond your control, like when to breathe, or blink your eyes. Others are very conscious, like when to clean the house. Then there are a bunch of choices that sit somewhere in the middle, like when to go to the toilet, or when and what to eat. With these last examples it's a bit trickier to say they are entirely conscious choices because there are other factors affecting your mind. You may not be consciously thinking about when you need the toilet, but at some point you have to make a conscious decision to go to the bathroom. Have you ever eaten an entire packet of biscuits (cookies) and not remembered anything past the first bite? Whether we are conscious of doing so or not, we are constantly choosing.

In some ways I had a slightly odd upbringing. My father was a thinker. He always described himself as a 'student of Buddhism' and he was a great fan of Zen teachings. I remember him telling me often (usually when I was in trouble) that I always have a choice about the action I take. "Even if someone were pointing a gun at your head", he would say, "you have a choice on what you do". To be honest, as a young child I really had no idea what he was talking about. My mind would go off... "Who would be putting a gun to my head? I live in England, we don't have guns" (at least not back then). As an adult working in the arena of positive psychology and human potential, I now realise that the idea that we are always at choice has proven to be very important in my learning and teaching. Thanks Dad.

It may be hard for you to hear this, especially if your life has involved people putting guns to your head, either in reality or emotionally, but you always do have a choice. I fully understand that it may not feel like much of a choice, but there is always choice. It is your ability to choose that will change your life experience as you change your mind.

Stop and take a breath.

What are you thinking right now?

If your mind has gone off on a rampage about what a load of old rubbish you are reading, and how you *know* there have been situations in your life over which you had *no choice,* and clearly this writer doesn't have a clue what she's talking about... If that's where your mind is, take a breath and say to yourself, "thanks for these thoughts, but what if there is another possibility?"

You see, I get it. As I got a bit older and my Dad would give me the 'choices' lecture, I *knew* he was talking rubbish (you remember what it was like to be a teenager). When I think back to challenging times in my life, *I never thought I had choices.* I lived from a place of victimhood and much of the time I was afraid, depressed and deeply unhappy.

I *now* know that all our mental chatter is about 'belief'. Your life so far has taught you what you think you know. It has taught you that everything you see around you is solid and that you are powerless to change your circumstances. It has taught you that you 'should' do this or that to be accepted in your family, job, or by society. One way or another you have probably learned that being different is not acceptable. But what if there are other possibilities?

To think positively is a great idea, it really is. And yet for most of us, before we train our minds, it is a virtual impossibility to do all of the time, or even most of the time. After some training it is still a practice which needs reminders and tools to keep your mind where you choose it to be. It does get easier, and in my life and the lives of many others I know, there was a tipping point, after which the forgetful occasions become fewer and fewer. It's not magic, it's available to everyone and all you need is to *be.*

The early ideas around positive thinking that I encountered on my journey were all about thinking happy thoughts, only focussing on the *good* thoughts and stopping the *bad* thoughts. The 'New Age' tag was added to positive thinking somewhere along the line and many logical, right-thinking people dismissed it as 'Pollyanna nonsense'. Some research came out that told us all this positive thinking had created a generation of selfish layabouts and another piece of research came along which said thinking positively can lengthen your life. These all may be true, it's really about what you believe, how those beliefs serve you, and whether you choose to hold onto those beliefs or not. Just like the idea of cats we talked about earlier - your belief creates the experience you have, there is no fundamental right or wrong.

On any subject you care to name there are myriad differing opinions, and evidence to prove all of them. Here's a story that speaks well to the idea of proving a particular belief:

In 1908 in the remote forested Siberian region of Tunguska, Russia, there was a huge explosion followed by a massive fire. It was devastating to the region and there was no apparent reason for it. Although there had been several expeditions to the area over the years, nothing had been discovered that could answer the tricky question of what had caused the explosion. A hundred years after the event, a collection of scientists decided to investigate exactly what had happened. The team of scientists included people with the following areas of expertise with their associated theories on what had caused this catastrophic explosion:

- An Astrophysicist with the theory that an asteroid had exploded over the land. He was looking for certain types of rocks.

- A Physicist with the theory that *Dark Matter* had caused the explosion. He was taking core samples of surviving trees, looking for a particular type of radiation.

- A Geophysicist who believed that a sudden and very rare type of volcanic burst called a *Wells Burst* had caused the incident. He was looking for rocks with particular properties.

- A Geologist who theorised that it was a meteorite landing on the earth that had created the explosion and the subsequent fire. He was looking for a crater.
- Finally there was an older gentleman who firmly believed that the entire incident had in some way been caused by aliens and their UFO. He was looking for anything that appeared to be of extraterrestrial manufacture.

The reason for sharing this story is not to have a great drum roll and tell you what the ultimate cause of this cataclysmic event actually was. It is to illustrate the power of belief that may have affected the scientists in finding the evidence they were looking for to support their particular theory. Who do you think was most likely to find evidence? Could it be the UFO hunter, the geophysicist, or perhaps the astrophysicist?

The amazing thing about this story is that *all* of them found *evidence* to support their personal theory, or *belief*. Even the ET guy found some evidence to support his theory.

I love this story as it speaks so well to the power of belief. If you hold strongly enough to a belief it will always be true for you. The question to ask is, "Does this belief support me?" Just like young Joe in our earlier story, is it possible that you are still clinging to old beliefs that no longer add value to your life?

It doesn't matter what you currently believe about positive thinking, the world around you, or your ability to change your current set of life circumstances. If you will follow the invitations in this book, and do the exercises and practises that are presented, you will start to experience changes and improvements. I can't promise an instant transformation, but I am certain that if you take the action and set your own intention to permanently practise changing your thoughts and re-training your mind, you will be well on your way to igniting success beyond beliefs, stepping into your greatest yet to be, and living a life beyond your dreams.

Your brain is like modelling clay

> *"The brain is not, as was thought, like a machine, or 'hardwired' like a computer. It is a plastic, living organ that can actually change its own structure and function, even into old age."*
> ~ NORMAN DOIDGE, M.D., FROM THE OFFICIAL WEBSITE
>
> OF *'THE BRAIN THAT CHANGES ITSELF'*

In the last twenty or thirty years science has made some amazing discoveries about all sorts of things. One of the most relevant to our conversation is that our brain is not fixed, ever. My oldest student is in his nineties and he is still rewiring his brain by changing his thoughts, words and deeds, and so can you.

As a child you may have heard words such as dumb, stupid, useless, idiot, and similar words that put people down. These may or may not have been directly targeted at you, yet you might have absorbed them into your belief system. Either way, guess what... they're not true. What is true is that you have an amazingly powerful brain which is constantly firing in all kinds of directions. It is a brain that you can change at any age. It is not limited in any way. Each one of us has a similar set of neurons and electrons, and we get to decide how to think. Some of us have a natural aptitude towards art, or maths, music or engineering. None of those aptitudes are better or worse, they are simply different. Each one as unique as your fingerprint, as unique as you are.

> *"The most important choice you make is what you choose to make important."*
>
> ~ MICHAEL NEILL

Bring your awareness back to the exercise you did at the end of chapter two. Think about those ideas of success you wrote down. Now you know your brain can be wired and rewired, and that nothing in your mind is set in stone, do you think about success any differently? And what about all those beliefs you came up with in chapter three? As far as your brain is concerned, they are all temporary electrical circuits, not the least bit permanent. More importantly, you can actively change your brain by very deliberately changing your thoughts and actions. As we saw from Amy Cuddy, moving your body in a certain way can change the chemistry in your body. With enough repetition, this will create new pathways in the brain, which in turn will create new behaviour, leading to new experiences.

Thinking makes it so

When I first came across some of these ideas I started off by using my mind to create parking spaces - perhaps you have too. If these ideas are completely new to you, you may be wondering why anyone would bother using their amazingly powerful mind to create a parking space. Have you ever been running late for an important appointment? Being able to mentally book ahead the perfect parking space is a great asset. Even after all these years, when I have my Mother in the car she will tell me how difficult it is to park in a certain place, yet we'll roll into the car park and slip directly into the perfect space, front and centre. Joking aside, one of the reasons we find creating parking spaces easy is that we usually don't have any mental attachment to getting one. There is no *need.* The opposite end of that idea is asking someone to create the money to pay their rent or mortgage at the end of the month. Which is something we have a lot more attachment to, so it is harder to achieve in our own minds. In terms of the actual creation, there is no difference. It is in our ability to believe something is possible that the challenge comes.

Every Monday I lead a Meditation group in my home town. We

usually meditate for about 45 minutes, spend a few minutes discussing our experience, and then we talk about the kinds of things I am speaking about in this book. One day the subject of parking spaces came up and my friend Lianne, who at the time was completely new to these ideas, asked what on earth we were talking about. I explained that by imagining a parking space right where you want it to be, having a sense of *knowing* the space is there waiting for you to arrive and then letting the thought go in total trust that the space will be there when you are, you will find that space easily, usually first time (occasionally I have had to drive around twice). When I told her this she was somewhat skeptical, but still open to the possibility. The following week she came into class all excited and she told us this story:

"Well, after what you had said about the parking space, on the way home I decided there would be a space outside my house. You have to understand, I live in a cul-de-sac, there's never any parking outside my house after five o'clock. But I decided, I just knew, there would be a space outside my house. And you won't believe it, I turned into my road, and there was a space, right outside my house. I went in and said to my husband, 'you'll never guess where I parked... right outside the house'. He couldn't believe it, there's never a parking space outside our house." Her excitement was infectious and her amazement clearly evident.

Lianne is one of my best students, largely because even when she thinks I'm a bit mad or totally spooky, she tries these things out and makes them work for herself. And you can too. Don't simply take my word for anything I tell you. Get out and do your own experimentation. When you gain your own body of evidence you get to 'embody' the teaching. It makes it so much easier to stay with it when you can call on your own experiences and truth.

There is no order of difficulty in miracles

This title is taken from a book called 'A Course In Miracles'. It speaks to the idea that within the Universal force or energy, there is no difference between creating a parking space or creating the rent money. The difficulty lies in our ability to believe it.

Reprogramming the way our minds work is as easy as we allow it to be. Time and time again students will tell me *it's hard* and I will remind them that every thought and word is an affirmation or a prayer or a rocket of desire that is being ushered forth into the creative medium. The more we claim how hard something is, the harder it seems to be.

When I was ten years old I loved the music of James Galway; he played the flute and I wanted to play the flute. I wanted to play the flute very much, and even though other people would tell me how hard it is to learn, I started lessons and found it so easy that in no time at all I was playing well enough to perform in front of others.

A year later I started to learn French in school. I had zero interest in learning French, I didn't see any value in it and it was *too hard* for me to learn. So three years of French classes resulted in lots of moaning and incomplete homework from me, three very frustrated teachers, and about twenty words of French being retained in my memory, most of which are not suitable for polite conversation.

When we believe something is easy and it interests us we will achieve it with what feels like almost no effort. If we believe something is hard then every step towards it will feel like we are dragging our tired bodies up a long, steep hill.

Remember that quote from Henry Ford - *"Whether you think you can or think you can't, you're right."* That's how the Universe works, it responds to what you think and what you think is based on beliefs that might be mistaken.

$E=mc^2$ and other strangeness

Physics was not my favourite subject in my high school

curriculum. I sat at the back and frequently didn't understand what the teacher was telling us. I'm not sure if this particular revelation was even taught, but if it was, I missed it. Consequently I was in my thirties before I understood what $E=mc^2$ actually means. When I discovered the answer I was as excited as a four-year-old blowing out candles on a birthday cake.

The simple translation of $E=mc^2$ is that matter (the physical stuff like your book or computer) and energy (things like electricity that you can't see) can swap about almost randomly. Fixed visible particles (stuff) can go back to being invisible energy and different forms of invisible energy can take form into stuff. Wow. As you can see I am no 'Doctor Quantum', but it is important to at least get a vague idea of this concept because it explains how our thoughts and feelings create nothing into something.

What this means is that everything we think of as *real* is just invisible energy moving (vibrating or *resonating*) in such a way that when we experience it, it looks, sounds and feels solid and very real.

I'm a simple person, I like to break things down into easy ways of understanding, and I get that this idea, especially if you have never given it a moment's attention, can be a bit mind boggling. Nothing real actually exists in the way we think it does. Everything, at its core, is made of vibrating bundles of energy - even your physical body. *And,* when you put your *focussed attention* on something, you can make it appear or disappear. This is called *the observer effect:* when you bring your attention to something, it changes.

I think this is how and why the many forms of spiritual - or faith-healing can work so effectively (or not). When the mind of the practitioner and the mind of the patient come together in one focussed thought, healing must occur. If there is an absence of focus or belief in the possibility of healing, either from the practitioner or the client, then healing is often slower or may not happen at all.

There are many books that will take you into the heady concept of quantum science; I have added some of my favourites into the bibliography at the back of this book. However, if you are eager to learn more about the science that sits behind these basic ideas, my favourite source of information is the movie 'What The Bleep Do We Know'. It has a great cartoon character called Dr. Quantum who takes it back to basics and explains all this stuff, the weirdness and what it means in the real world. The movie has lots of content so you may need to watch it in parts, or a few times, to get the hang of it, but if you want to learn more about these ideas, *What The Bleep* is my best recommendation.

Change your thinking, change your life

Here's what I know; our minds are constantly thinking, and those thoughts are creating things and experiences in our lives. It is possible for us to train our brains to think more positively, more creatively, and far more effectively. If we take the time to learn how to train our brains we can have happier, more peaceful, more fulfilled lives. So why wouldn't we all want to do that?

When you read it out like that it makes perfect sense that everyone in the world would be clamouring for this information. On some level they are, which is why a book and movie called 'The Secret' sold over 19 million copies a few years back. But when it comes to taking the action and making *lasting* changes, it is our old friend *Belief* who stands in the way.

By the time we are seven we have all, on some level, decided how the world will support us. As adults, the subconscious mind keeps trying to prove us right by subtly creating situations that bring forth evidence so that we can say, "See, I knew that would happen, that's my *destiny*." Or we blame the guy in the sky and say, "It's God's will for my life."

I believe the two things the God of my understanding (Universe,

Source, Gaia) wants for us is happiness and love, and the only things that are destined in our lives are the ones we decide to agree on with ourselves.

Chapter 4 Awareness Exercise - Where are you now?

Take a moment to close your eyes and imagine taking an audit or stock check of your life so far. Think of all the things you have experienced, good, bad and in between. Now look at the statements below and decide how true they are for you right now on a scale from 1 to 10, with 1 being "I don't even want to think of it, it's so bad" and 10 being "wow it can't get better than this". The more honest you are with yourself, the more useful this exercise will be for you.

a. When I wake up in the morning I am excited and delighted to be alive.

    1   2   3   4   5   6   7   8   9   10

b. I love doing what I do all day.

    1   2   3   4   5   6   7   8   9   10

c. I feel fulfilled in every area of my life.

    1   2   3   4   5   6   7   8   9   10

d. I live in balance and harmony with my money.

    1   2   3   4   5   6   7   8   9   10

e. I have great relationships with everyone in my circles.

    1   2   3   4   5   6   7   8   9   10

f. My body is vibrant, fit, healthy and well.

    1   2   3   4   5   6   7   8   9   10

g. I feel happy and optimistic when I think about my future.

    1   2   3   4   5   6   7   8   9   10

h. When I experience a challenge I have people in my life who will help lift me up.

    1   2   3   4   5   6   7   8   9   10

i. I have a personal spiritual connection or faith that serves and supports me.

    1   2   3   4   5   6   7   8   9   10

j. When I think about my life I feel confident, safe and empowered.

1   2   3   4   5   6   7   8   9   10

Always remembering that this is an *awareness* exercise. It is designed to help you know yourself better and to understand where you are today.

Where are you now?

Your score is a piece of information indicating where you are today in regard to the level of optimism and positive thinking in your life. It is not good or bad, right or wrong. It is simply a reference point on an arbitrary scale so that you can recognise improvements next time you check your progress.

If you add up all your numbers you will have a total score out of 100. This is useful as a reference point to see where you are now. When you come back to do it next time you will have a clear indicator of the improvements you have made.

I have discovered in my own life that I don't always take time to recognise the improvements I have made in my life. Most of us have not been taught to see and celebrate our successes. This tool will allow you to do that for yourself.

Going Beyond Positive Thinking

Chapter 5

IMAGINATION ISN'T JUST FOR KIDS

"Go confidently in the direction of your dreams. Live the life you have imagined."

~ HENRY DAVID THOREAU

Foundation 2

Imagination: My imagination is the most creative part of my mind so I allow myself to dream big.

You, like me, may have been told off as a child for daydreaming. I distinctly remember hearing one of my teachers say, "Wasting your time daydreaming won't get you anywhere in life, you have to work hard to get what you want." This same message was reinforced at home. I was regularly told that I was too trusting, too easily upset, and too easily lost in my imagination. My inner translation of all this feedback was that I was weak, soft and stupid. So, at seventeen, I packed away my childish dreams, focussed on 'reality' and joined the Women's Royal Naval Service. I can assure you, basic training was definitely not a place where imagination was encouraged.

The great thing about imagination is that it never goes away. We may think we have stuffed it into a dim and distant corner of our minds or mentally hidden it under a pile of dirty laundry, but the truth is it's running rampant through our minds each and every day. Don't believe me? Try this on for size: Pretend for a moment that last week you had a conversation with a friend that resulted in a difference of opinion where neither of you could see the other person's viewpoint and you left feeling irritated and incomplete. Take a moment to consider the possible outcomes from this encounter:

- How much time would you subsequently spend running and re-running that conversation through your mind over and over again, thinking about what you could have, or should have said?
- How often would you think about that conversation and make up stories about your friend and why they didn't understand what you were saying?
- How many times would you replay the original conversation and once again become irritated about your friend's lack of understanding?

What's really happening here?

I'm sure you have had many situations similar to this. After the original conversation, everything else is happening in your imagination. It's not real, it's not actually happening when you are thinking about it. You are making it all up. However, as you bring your thoughts into the now moment, what physical sensations do they create in your body? Do you feel the stress and anxiety physically? What about the feelings of irritation and frustration, how do they show up in your body? Whenever you think about a certain thing (either a memory or something fresh from your imagination) and it creates physical sensations in your body, you are creating something from nothing. The thought is formless, it only exists in your mind. The sensation has a physical appearance, either pain and discomfort, or relaxation and well being, depending on the kind of thought you are focussed on.

Have you ever been out for a meal with friends only to discover that you don't have any money with you when the bill comes? You accidentally left your purse or wallet at home and you have no money. What stories do you immediately start to make up? Are you worrying about what your friends or the restaurant staff might think about you? Do you find yourself falling into self-criticism about being stupid and forgetful? As a result of these different thoughts, do you find your physical body reacting? Perhaps you get a little hot and flushed, or perhaps your stomach starts to churn a little. You may have some, all, or none of these responses. The important thing to recognise is that they are all happening in your mind. None of the stories are real, they are all a result of your rich and fertile imagination.

If you're like me, then hopefully you are smiling in recognition of how much you do this in many everyday situations. You see, it is impossible not to have your imagination actively working. Our minds are designed to think. The challenge for us humans is to stop using them to unconsciously terrorise and upset ourselves. Instead, it better serves us to master our imaginations so that we can deliberately use them to create the experiences we want. How often do you notice you are mentally terrorising yourself by running off into the future with thoughts of what might happen? How do you feel when you do that? Now that you are more aware of the power of your mind I'm sure you'll get better and better at catching yourself and bringing your awareness back to your body in the infinite now. After all, how often have you spent time scaring yourself about something only to have it turn out wonderfully? It's time to practise focussing your mind on the good you want to experience. That way you'll feel better much more of the time.

We have already seen that on some level our thoughts affect

'stuff' or *matter* and bring things into this material world. Applying this concept to the 'friends conversation' example above, can you imagine how the relationship might be detrimentally affected by all the thought energy we invest in re-running the conversation, and re-experiencing the feelings? In addition, what do you think is happening in our bodies when we get knots in our stomachs because we created a story about what others think about us when we don't have the money to pay for our meal? It's time to release the drama of life, and stop using your mind to frighten yourself. Now is the time to embrace these ideas so that we can create the peace, happiness and fulfillment we really want.

Imagination is pregnant with potential

> *"Imagination is the ability to create an idea, a mental picture, or a feeling sense of something. In creative visualization you use your imagination to create a clear image, idea, or feeling of something you wish to manifest."*
>
> ~ SHAKTI GAWAIN

Imagination, as you can see, is so much more than the things we learned about as children. Hidden within imagination lies the entire realm of infinite potential. Without imagination nothing would exist in the material world because everything starts with a concept or idea birthed in the rich and fertile ground of one's imagination.

I want to add a little something here before we rush on. I referred to *infinite potential*, and I want to be sure you catch this phrase in the web of your mind. It gets bandied around quite a bit these days and it's easy to skip over it without really engaging our brains to the magnitude of this concept.

Have you ever seen one of those pictures from deep space looking back at planet earth and showing it as a tiny pin prick of light with an arrow and a caption that reads "You are here"? If not, check in with your favourite search engine and have a look. An image like that, depicting the vastness of the universe, allows me to get my head around the concept of *infinity*. Infinite potential means that anything and everything is available to us. Take a breath and really open your mind to the hugeness of this concept. Within your imagination is everything that ever is, was, or will be. The only thing that limits the *infinite possibility* within you is your belief in what's possible. Take another breath. This is massive. You can be, do, or have anything. There are no limits inside your imagination. Keep breathing - remember, we decided earlier, breathing's essential.

So what's next?

As cave people we decided that we no longer wanted to sit on the floor on skins, so someone brought a tree stump into the cave, and so the first chair was created. It is said that, 'necessity is the mother of all invention', which is probably true in the first part of the creative process, but what happens next? A tree stump, resting against the wall of a cave with a bear skin thrown over it, makes a perfectly good chair. What happens in the evolving human mind to get us from tree stump to the finest Chippendale chair? It's not so much need, as imagination.

Our uniqueness allows each of us to activate our imagination differently. Thomas Chippendale's furniture designs could only have come from his imagination, even though many great cabinet makers copied his designs. George Lucas used his imagination to bring us Star Wars. Gandhi used his imagination to liberate an entire country peacefully. What is waiting to be born through your unique imagination? Are you ready to set it free?

I believe that we all have *dreams:* things that we have imagined, or thought up. You may have things that come into your imagination as you read a book or magazine. What about the things that inspired you in school? Or even things that upset you in the world and that you want to change, and make a difference about? We have these thoughts, and then our beliefs about what is possible come crashing down like a tidal wave and wash them away. But just like the aftermath of a tidal wave, everything gets washed up eventually. Your dreams never go away, they get pushed aside until you are ready to remember.

What are your long-forgotten dreams?

> *"All our dreams can come true, if we*
> *have the courage to pursue them."*
>
> ~ WALT DISNEY

What grand possibilities did you imagine as a child, then pack away and forget because someone told you they were 'pie in the sky' nonsense?

Take a moment to breathe into this question. There is often a clue in the things you loved to play with as a child, or the jobs you imagined having. These possibilities have not gone away. They have lain dormant waiting patiently for you to remember who you are and how powerful your mind is.

Opening or re-opening your mind to greater creativity is something that you can improve through learning and practise. It also needs time. The idea of sitting in a chair and doing nothing for 30 minutes may seem unnecessary to you. You may have thoughts like: How silly to sit and do nothing; I don't have time; I have too many other things to do; I would feel lazy sitting doing nothing.

I have heard all these *beliefs* and many more besides. Perhaps you are thinking some or all of these, perhaps not. Either way, if you want to change your life, you need to change your habits. Making time to sit still, without any interruptions or distractions, and allowing your mind to daydream is a vitally important tool for transformation. The sages of old would call this *contemplation* and it could be considered a spiritual practice. No matter what you call it, I invite you to do it. Make time, ideally every day, to sit and breathe and do nothing. Allow your mind to wander where it will for a while and then invite in a question. Perhaps your first question could be, "What do I love?" As you start to discover answers to this question you may find your ability to imagine greater possibilities for your life will increase and you will be better able to conceive greater levels of success.

What do you believe about what you can conceive?

This little equation is simple, and yet incredibly powerful when it comes to igniting your success.

$$C + B = A$$

where

$$C = \text{Conceive}; B = \text{Believe}; A = \text{Achieve}$$

Conceive

Just like our tree stump chair, you need to be able to imagine something (conceive it) first. Without that first thought or idea you have nothing to build on.

Then…

Believe

It's no good imagining something totally amazing if that voice inside your head doesn't think it's possible (you don't believe). All your wishes and dreams are worthless if they are washed away by the tidal wave of your doubts and fears.

When you bring together the idea and the belief in that idea, then...

Achieve

When you have strong and lasting belief in the dreams and imaginings of your mind, you will achieve them. I can't guarantee when, but if there is passion in your imagination and strong belief about the possibilities, those two things will create amazing energy that will inspire you to action and create seeming miracles in the *coincidences* of how everything comes into being.

Remember - coincidence is when the Infinite Intelligence within you wants to remain anonymous.

The practice of imagining

I'd like you to imagine that you are stroking a very happy and contented big, fat, white, fluffy cat sitting on a luxurious deep pile red rug. Close your eyes and allow your imagination to create that idea in your mind.

Depending on your brain's preference for processing, you may have *seen* a very clear image of the cat on the mat in your mind's eye. You may have *heard* the cat purring. You may have imagined the *feel* of the cat's silky fur on your hand, or the softness of the deep pile rug. You may have had a *knowing* of the image without any of the other sensory input. As we already discussed, you are perfectly unique and your brain has a preference for how it receives and processes information. This is an important thing to remember because we are now going into the realm of creative visualisation.

I have long since decided that creative *visualisation* is wrongly named. A far more accurate title for the practice I am about to explain would be creative *imaginisation*. As you experienced from imagining the cat on the mat, it is not only your inner ability to visualise an image that gets used. All your senses are deployed in different ways. You may have even been aware of a particular smell whilst bringing the cat on the mat picture to your mind. Although your mind may have a preference for either seeing, hearing, feeling or knowing, it is possible to develop all of these areas through practise, and that's just what I have in mind: more practise.

"Creative visualization can be an effective tool for healing because it goes straight to the source of the problem -- your own mental concepts and images."

SHAKTI GAWAIN, *CREATIVE VISUALIZATION*

I have always thought that if it is possible for *someone* to learn *something*, then it is possible for me to learn that same thing. It doesn't mean that I *will* learn it, it just means that with the right level of motivation, I *could*. I invite you to take the same approach if that voice in your head is still stuck on the loop of "I can't visualise". Your amazing brain can be rewired through a process, and if you are sufficiently motivated, this is one such process.

Think of this as an experiment. Every day, for an entire month, I invite you to spend five minutes using your rich and fertile imagination to create an experience in your mind of a specific thing that you want. Perhaps that is a new car, a particular pair of expensive shoes, getting through a morning without feeling pain in your body, or waking up in the morning without a sense of dread for the day ahead. It doesn't matter what the thing or experience is. What matters is that you use *all* your senses to imagine it into reality.

I live part of my life in Southern California, and I have many people there that I love and want to spend time with. Here's an example of the kind of creative imaginisation I might do to draw forth the perfect place to stay for three months when I am visiting:

Sitting comfortably, in a relaxed state of mind, with no external interruptions, I allow my mind to soften and think of Laguna Beach, my favourite place in Southern California. I imagine myself walking along the boardwalk, feeling the sun on my skin, the gentle sea breeze in my hair, and wrapped in the salty aroma. I imagine the sound of the gulls as I watch them swoop and soar. Next I envision seeing a flight of dragonflies hovering about the greenery and hearing the car horns honk as impatient drivers get frustrated with the thronging people cluttering the street. I imagine delighting in a sumptuous meal at my favourite restaurant with a group of visiting friends, then all of us taking a walk down on the beach through my favourite little cove.

Eventually, I imagine walking along the beach to some steps that lead up to a fabulous beachfront property, bounding up the steps in my usual high energy way, and opening the patio doors and entering into a beautifully decorated 3-bedroom, 4-bathroom home. The kitchen would be fully equipped with a juicer, Vitamix and tea kettle (a must for this Englishwoman). In the sitting room there would be a fireplace for the cooler evenings, as well as a fire pit built into the patio. The cosy sitting room has plenty of space for everyone to be comfortable and there is a large dining space for an abundance of great food. I would imagine the conversations, the food, the vibrant juices and smoothies, the peace, and the sound of the ocean just beyond the patio. Then I would imagine resting in a comfy-cozy bed and drifting into dream time. Then I would be done - I wouldn't dwell on how I might make it happen, that's not my business. Mine is to imagine so well that for those five minutes it is completely real. Then I let it go.

Do you see how I used my entire body to feel, hear, see and know this experience? For me *hearing* is my primary modality, with *knowing* (or intention) second. In fact *seeing* or *visualisation* is my brain's least favoured data processing tool, so I don't necessarily *see* an image in my mind's eye, I *know* an image because I have a reference for what Laguna Beach looks like, what the beachfront properties are like, and how I feel when I'm there.

As I always say, "It's a practice." It doesn't matter what you want to experience or create. If you practise this five-minute process of *creative visualisation* every day, you will start to see things appearing in your world. Remember, it's an experiment - any results you get are just results, not good or bad, right or wrong, just results that will inform your next experiment.

If you want to dive deeper into this technique, one of my favourite books on the subject, and probably the best known in the world, is 'Creative Visualization' by Shakti Gawain. It is brilliant and simple and a really great place to take your knowledge and skills deeper.

There really are no limits

Let's dive a bit deeper into this idea that your powerful imagination really can create anything because I know how much this can boggle our limited belief system.

When I say that you can create *anything* in your imagination, that's really what I mean. I think this is best illustrated in films. Think of the vast array of film genres people make. I personally like romantic comedies, children's cartoons, some of the kids' action adventure stuff, and some science fiction. One of my friends loves horrors movies, and another likes thrillers, neither of which I would ever watch. No matter what kind of films you happen to enjoy, think for a moment about the imagination that has to go into creating a film.

In 2009, James Cameron brought out the first Avatar film. It was cutting-edge at the time for the technology it used, and in many ways it was the Star Wars of its age. Although we can look around the universe and see where some of the inspiration for the story came from, lots of pieces were pure imagination. It's worth noting that James Cameron had the original idea back in 1994, and the finished film didn't release until 2009. Sometimes it can take a while for our imaginings to come into fruition in this physical realm.

So, back to what you could imagine. I have found, in my own life, that using my imagination, just like using a muscle, gets easier the more I practise. Just like going to a gym and working out, our imagination strengthens and grows as we train and practise.

Here's a list of things that could be imagined. Depending on what is current in your life, some will be relevant and some won't. Have a read through them to see which you could believe in and which you couldn't. Always remembering that there is no right or wrong. This is all about expanding your awareness. Which of these could you imagine?

- Feeling a greater sense of peace and calm in your life
- Increasing your monthly income by 500 a month
- Meeting the partner of your dreams
- Being debt free
- Feeling relaxed and trusting that all your bills are paid
- Being totally pain-free forever
- Being completely healed from *whatever* your diagnosis is
- Having the car of your dreams
- Making time to sit still, breathe, and imagine a better life
- Creating lasting change in your eating habits so that you nourish your body fully
- Being totally caffeine free
- Getting up every morning feeling excited to be alive
- Feeling a complete sense of fulfillment within your career or vocation
- Owning your own home, free and clear
- Becoming a Nobel Prize winner
- Feeling safe every day

- Living a life filled with passion and purpose
- Living every moment filled with a deep sense of love

As I said, some of these will be a resounding 'Yes', some will be a hopeless 'No', some will be a wobbly 'maybe' and others will not even have any meaning to you. No right or wrong, good or bad - it's another opportunity for awareness.

Every item on this list *could* be imagined into being. If you were passionate enough and a specific thing had meaning in your life, you could imagine it and bring it forth into creation. My current dream car has just changed from a Maserati Quattroporte to a Tesla Model S, in yellow of course. As I have only just discovered the Model S I haven't yet been on the website, specified all the trim, gadgets and colours, but I will. I have long had a picture of 'my' Quattroporte on the wall of my office, and I still wouldn't turn it down if someone drove up to the house, knocked on the door and handed me the keys. I have simply moved into wanting something that looks sexy *and* is eco-friendly.

My dream car is not the highest priority on my creation list, but I regularly spend some time *day-dreaming* about driving it, feeling the wooden steering wheel in my hands as I glide around country roads, smelling that new car smell enhanced by the delightful odour of tanned leather, enjoying the excellent sound quality from the stereo. With the Tesla Model S the one thing I won't be hearing is the roar of an engine as it's all electric, but I'm sure I'll find some other sounds to ignite my auditory senses.

A fancy car is a relatively easy thing to imagine. Some of the other things on the list maybe absolutely beyond your ability right now, and that's okay. You are in the process of becoming your greatest yet to be and this is only one of the steps. Allow your mind to open to the idea of *infinite potential,* even if that voice inside your head is busy telling you it's not possible.

Chapter 5 Awareness Exercise - Flexing your imagination muscle

Okay, now it's time for you to play with this idea. Pick something that you would love to be, do or have. Just for now pick only one thing and use all your senses to imagine what it would be like, how you would feel, what your different senses would bring forth when you experience the delivery of this thing. If you need to, go back and re-read the section on using *all* of your senses. Allow it to be a full body experience and let it become as real as it possibly can.

Practise this every day and watch for the voice of your belief system telling you things like 'what a waste of time' or 'you don't deserve that'. Our belief system is powerful, any time you find yourself in that chatter mode, simply say, 'thank you for sharing, I know you are trying to keep me safe, we are experimenting with something new, so you can take a rest, I am safe'.

I invite you to make this a daily practice and look out for evidence that the good is revealing. Let me know how you get on. I'd love to hear about it.

Chapter 6

FEELINGS ARE LIKE ROCKET FUEL

*"Your feelings create the pattern
from which your world is
fashioned, and a change of feeling
is a change of pattern."*

~ NEVILLE GODDARD

Foundation 3

**Feelings: The feelings I add to my thoughts
provide jet fuel for my mental creations.**

We have feelings for a reason. How in touch are you with yours? I have to say I have sometimes wondered at their usefulness when I have been sobbing my heart out at the loss of a loved one. Our feelings, when we have a healthy relationship with them, are our very own personal guidance system. Like having a permanent internal satellite navigation (SatNav) system or GPS. The tricky thing about emotions is that the way we process them internally and the way we express them externally has been significantly affected by our upbringing and the resulting belief system we have adopted. Therefore we may not be in a healthy relationship with *all* of our feelings.

In this book I use emotions and feelings interchangeably. There are some occasions where I have differentiated between emotional feelings and physical feelings such as touch when describing the use of all our senses for creative imaginisation. Emotional awareness is recognising that you are experiencing a certain feeling. Through the effective use of emotional awareness we can develop our feeling nature to help guide us along the path of our life. You don't have to be at the whim of your emotional feelings. They are available to you as part of your natural guidance system. They are a feedback loop for the things you experience in life; letting you know what feels good and what feels not so good. Mastering your feelings goes hand-in-hand with mastering your mind. As you become more in tune with your thoughts and the beliefs that empower them, you will be better able to recognise how your feelings guide you to the best kinds of experiences.

I have found it incredibly annoying, on occasions, that I can't switch off my feelings. Even back in the days when I suppressed and denied them, I still couldn't switch them off. Have you ever wanted to stop the pain of a broken heart? Or switch off the rage that could move you to violence? Have you ever wished that the all consuming fear paralysing you in the darkest hours of the night could be eradicated forever with a smile? I have.

I tried for many years to ignore, stuff-down, deny, eliminate and otherwise cast out as useless the feelings I experienced. I never managed it. I did manage to drive myself into greater and greater depths of stress, anxiety and depression until I was finally broken open and washed clean by the floodgates of almost forty years of unexpressed emotions.

That might seem a scary prospect. For me it was a liberation - undoubtedly the best thing that has ever happened to me. Was it an easy process to go through? No. Was it worth every tear and every punched pillow? Hell yes. If I hadn't been able to go through that process I wouldn't be sitting here writing this book. I would still be uptight and miserable, believing I knew everything and that the world owed me a living.

Take a breath. How are *you* feeling after reading these few paragraphs?

- Does it feel uncomfortable to read and think about emotions?
- How were emotions handled in your family, as you were growing up?
- Do you have a healthy relationship with your emotions?
- Could this subject be an opportunity for growth and learning in your life?

> *"Owning our story can be hard but not nearly as*
> *difficult as spending our lives running from it."*
>
> ~ BRENÉ BROWN

These are wise words indeed. If you haven't heard of Brené Brown, I invite you to look her up. She is an amazing researcher and best-selling author who speaks about vulnerability, wholeheartedness and shame, amongst other things. Her books *The Gifts Of Imperfection* and *Daring Greatly* are on my essential reading list for all my clients.

I was raised in a fairly traditional English/South African way. The sweeping generalisation of the English 'stiff upper lip' is founded on a base of truth. I did not have strong role models for processing or expressing emotions when growing up. I *learned* that it was not okay for me to express anger or sadness, and that crying was a sign of weakness. No-one expressly *told* me those things, that was how I interpreted what I saw and heard around me. I then synthesised and adopted this into the operating system of my *beliefs*. Just like Joe in chapter three, I took subtle and not-so-subtle experiences and made up a story about what they meant. We are all doing that, all the time, but remember, thoughts and beliefs can be changed. I changed mine and I know, if you want to, you can change yours. Remember to keep breathing.

Clear water runs deep

We are going to explore our deeper *feelings* so you can start to understand the value and importance of them before I ask you to start actively using them as a tool to change your life. All your beliefs, hidden and obvious, hold emotional charge or a strength of feeling. Some are like a firefly, while some are like a nuclear reactor. It all depends on the circumstances under which they were formed. Just like the beliefs, these feelings hide in the layers of your infinite onion-like self. All you have to do is keep peeling if you want to uncover them and set yourself free.

Taking the journey to liberate some of these hidden feelings is just like dredging a pond to get rid of the overgrown weed. Once you clear some space, the light can get in and allow things to grow. In our case, the light also allows us to tap into our feelings in a healthy way and start to use them in support of our personal transformation. It can be difficult to use and trust our feelings as a navigation device when we have so many contradictory and confusing beliefs about them. That is why it is important, and very valuable, to be willing to excavate in our emotional mud, pull up the weeds of mistaken beliefs, and allow the light to shine through the clear waters of understanding. I promise you don't have to copy me and do it all at once. I have always been impatient and something of a speed demon, hence my childhood nickname of 'Jet'. It is important that you are gentle with yourself as you go on this journey. You may even want to use the support of a counsellor or therapist to help with the excavation.

When we harness the compass and passion of our *feelings* we can get clearer about what we want and we can ignite success with the speed of a rocket.

Emotions and the field

There is an amazing non-profit organisation called The Institute of HeartMath® (www.heartmath.org), based in Boulder Creek, California. (Just for my English readers, it would be HeartMathS if they were founded in the UK.) The wonderful people at HeartMath® have made it their mission to study the human heart, our emotions, how heart and emotional energy signals connect to, and interact with, the brain and how all that human energy impacts and influences the energy of the earth.

Our heart is the *feeling* centre of the body. Here are some facts from HeartMath® about the heart and its workings that you may not know:

- Your heart constantly puts out electromagnetic energy fields that change according to your emotions.
- This energy field can be measured several feet away from the body.
- Positive emotions create physical improvements in the body.
- You can even boost your immune system by invoking positive emotions.
- Negative emotions create chaos in the nervous system and positive emotions do the opposite.
- As babies developing in the womb, our hearts form and start beating before our brains develop.
- The heart sends more information to the brain than the brain sends to the heart.
- Positive emotions help the brain with creativity and innovative problem solving.
- Positive emotions can increase the brain's ability to make good decisions.

Before we continue with this valuable information and its

relevance to us in igniting success beyond beliefs, I just want to position the idea of *Positive* and *Negative* emotions and how they are used in this book. Fundamentally, emotions are neither *positive* or *negative*. They are feelings that inform us, as part of our emotional guidance system (internal SatNav), about whether we are going in a direction that supports our hopes and dreams or not. However, in the HeartMath® research, some feelings have been shown to have a positive effect on our body and brain and others a detrimental effect. It is based on these discoveries that the idea of *positive* or *negative* emotions is used here.

Here's an example of emotions that fall into the *Positive* group:

- Compassion
- Love
- Gratitude & appreciation
- Peace
- Joy
- Happiness

None of your emotions are good or bad, right or wrong. To believe that is like thinking that when the voice on your car's satellite navigation says, "when possible make a legal U turn" it's a bad thing. That would be silly. It's just telling you that you are off course and you might benefit from a change of direction. That's exactly what your feelings are doing for you.

So, back to feelings, the heart, and the brain

As we can see from the HeartMath® information, there is a lot going on in the heart with regard to our feelings and how they impact on the world around us. The fields of energy that come from the heart create a constant cloud around each one of us, something like our own miniature atmosphere. We are both transmitting and receiving information constantly as we bump into other energy fields and exchange information. That same energy is also going out into the ether and impacting on the energy of the earth and the universe.

You are so much more powerful that you knew. Your emotional energy is impacting the entire earth and beyond. If this interests you, and you would like to learn more about your personal atmosphere, I invite you to visit www.HeartMath.org and learn directly from their cutting edge research and information.

In the last twenty years positive psychology, the study of healthy brains and emotions, has taught us that we can increase the amount of positive emotions we experience in everyday life. It has been proven that if you want to move from being a half empty kind of person to an all the way full kind of person, it is absolutely possible to do so through a repeatable process of deliberate thought that is written down daily. This actually results in physically rewiring the brain.

In the last chapter we discovered how versatile your imagination really is. You learned that your imagination is constantly running rampant and you can harness it with *creative imaginisation* to bring forth the things you want in your life. Now that you know just how powerful your feelings are and that you can deliberately change your feelings to have a more positive bias, let's see how we use them like rocket fuel to achieve our greatest yet to be.

In the *Awareness Exercise* at the end of the last chapter I invited you to imagine something you wanted to be, do, or have. I encouraged you to use all of your physical senses to bring your imagination to life. Now think about that same thing and add to your imaginings a profound feeling of gratitude and appreciation for it. Then start feeling joyful delight that it is already yours. And just for good measure, imagine being super excited (like a small child on his or her birthday), rushing around telling the people that you love all about your good fortune to have this thing happen in your life. Allow yourself to dive into the feelings like an actor playing a part. You want the audience to believe you, so make your feelings as real as you can within yourself.

As you imagine doing that, take a breath and check in with your body. How does it feel? Do you recognise an increase in gratitude, joy and excitement? Are you feeling a bit of a buzz within your body?

In his book *Biology of Belief*, Bruce Lipton talks about the fact that the brain doesn't know the difference between something that it imagines, remembers, or is experiencing right now. Here's my rough translation of the above sentence: When you go through the imagination exercise above, your body *feels* the appreciation, joy, excitement and the love. It smells the smells, feels the physical feelings (like the touch of wood or leather), hears the sounds, even tastes the tastes if you are imagining have a great cup of coffee or eating garlic bread. Your body experiences all those things *as if* you were actually doing them. The way your brain and your body are wired is to physically experience everything in what I call *the infinite now*. It can't tell the difference because, on some level, it understands that there is no yesterday or tomorrow, there is only *now*.

Here's what I really like about all this: When you get very good at bringing your physical senses into alignment with your emotions, the things you are imagining can start to show up very quickly. You may still have some of those sneaky hidden beliefs that hold you back. This is why it is important to always be working on revealing and releasing them in some way. But combining the physical senses and the emotions into your creative imaginisation is like pouring rocket fuel into a firework and lighting the touch paper or fuse - stars and sparkles go off in all directions.

How good can you let it be?

Once upon a time, there was a baby girl called Sarah. She was given away to foster carers almost as soon as she was born. A few weeks later she was given away by the foster people to new people that she didn't know. Just like an adopted cat, she was finally in her forever home, but her baby brain didn't understand that. She had already made up a story about her life so far. It was immediately tucked away in the hidden part of her mind (the subconscious) and it went something like this:

If the person who gave birth to me didn't want me, and the next people didn't want me, there must be something very, very wrong with me. I must be totally unloveable and not enough in any way. I know that soon these new people will give me away and that people will always give me away because I am just not enough.

As adults we can understand and rationalise the process of adoption and can have total compassion for a mother's decision to give up her child into foster care. That's the adult rational brain. That rationality does not help to deal with the hidden beliefs about being unloveable and worthless that baby Sarah acquired into her subconscious mind.

This is my story, I was baby Sarah. And as an adult I am grateful for everything that happened in my life. But it took some time to discover these hidden beliefs and a little longer to liberate them. I share this because it is the best illustration I have in my own experience about the power of hidden beliefs. Perhaps you can imagine how good I became at running away from situations before people could *give me away* or *abandon* me. At the time I always believed that it was *them* that caused me to flee, but as I learned what I am describing in this book, I realised that it was all about me. The good news? I have changed my beliefs and set myself free, and so can you.

When it comes to using our powerful imaginations, combined with all our feeling senses, we can create almost anything. There is nothing in the Infinite Intelligence that is limited. It is only our beliefs (conscious and subconscious) about what's possible that can limit us.

How good can you allow your life to be?

Many of us talk about winning the lottery, being with the partner of our dreams, or retiring early and doing work for the good of others. But how many of us regularly use our imagination and feelings to create those things? Often we take the first step, but fall at the second hurdle because we don't actually believe it's possible for us.

Whatever you want to be, do, or have is possible for you. Whether you achieve it or not can be significantly impacted by these four things:

1. You keep visualising with all your feeling senses fully engaged.
2. You practise persistently and compassionately to uncover your hidden beliefs and rewire your mind.
3. You are truly passionate about achieving your desire.
4. You take consistent inspired action towards your goals.

This very book, the words you are reading right now, is a great example of the stop/start cycle that we fall into. I have been talking about and visualising my finished book for more than seven years. And although I wrote almost daily, I didn't get close to formulating a book because the voice inside my head was chattering away with doubt and fear. Once I decided that I would not let it define me and neither would I let it stop me, I found the process of writing much easier than I thought it could be. And trust me - if I can do it, anyone can. And that includes YOU.

I finally got finished with a full size book because:

1. I never stopped the imaginisation,
2. I consistently practise uncovering my hidden beliefs,
3. I am beyond passionate about what I teach, and
4. I got some help with the practicalities of writing a book - my inspired action was to hire a coach, in the form of

Dennis Merritt Jones (who is brilliant), and I allowed myself to be guided and supported through the process.

Back to the equation from our earlier conversation: C+B=A. If you can **Conceive** it, and then **Believe** it, you *can* **Achieve** it.

I know I keep repeating this, but you *can* achieve anything. Whether you *do* is about the action you take in these four areas.

Oh, and there is one other thing you would benefit from understanding. Sometimes the timing isn't quite where you want it to be. There is something in the Universe which is often called Divine Timing. Your inner knowing is connected to the Infinite Mind and sometimes something within you knows that there is a better moment for your good to be delivered.

Have you ever been really desperate to get a certain job, and when you didn't get it, you felt terribly disappointed? Then, just a few weeks later, a far better job comes along completely out of the blue and you are instantly grateful that you didn't get the first one. Have you ever been in that situation, or something similar? That's Divine Timing. You can only do your steps diligently, trusting the process of life to support you on the journey. The more you practise and see results, the easier it is to trust that process.

There is a great book by Pam Grout called E^2. In the book, Pam talks about setting a time line for delivery. That can work beautifully, *and,* sometimes *we* have to become the people we need to be in order to receive the good that we want. There is a risk that by setting a timescale and then not achieving it, you could become disillusioned and give up completely in the belief that you are not the creative force in your life. You may even fall back into believing that everything is pre-destined and that you are stuck in your life, just the way it is. So I would invite you to be cautious when setting timescales for delivery. It's good to not limit yourself, or the Infinite, in any way.

An example of this is my personal relationship with the love of my life. We were first introduced to each other in February 2009, but we didn't connect and start dating until August 2010. Once we got together and started talking about our lives, we both realised that neither of us had been ready for our relationship back in '09. We were still in the *process of becoming* who we needed to be. Trusting that there is something working *for* you can be a challenge sometimes, especially when it comes to relationships, money and health. I'm so glad that I trusted the process of life to bring me the perfect thing at the perfect time. I now have the kind of relationship that I never used to believe was possible. I am so very blessed and deeply grateful for my life with my beloved.

Here's an affirmation for you:

I can be, do, or have anything I desire.

Read and speak this out loud as often as you can.

If that feels totally false, and that voice inside your head is disagreeing with you, try this on for size:

I am willing to believe I can be, do, or have anything I desire right now.

We'll talk more about affirmations in chapter 8. But here is a quick introduction to the concept: An affirmation is a statement made in the first person ("I"), in the present moment ("now"), and in the affirmative or positive ("am", "have", "can", etc.). Stay away from using words like "will" or "not", "don't" and "no" because they take you away from the infinite now and continue to create whatever comes after the negative. For example, "I will no longer eat fast food", is not a useful affirmation because "will" indicates sometime off in the non-existent future and "no longer" doesn't work in the infinite intelligence; you are effectively declaring "I eat fast food." An affirmation that is more likely to create the change you seek would be something like this, "I always eat vibrant, nourishing, healthy food." We'll dive deeper later on, but for now... it's your turn.

Chapter 6 Awareness Exercise ~ The Feeling Tone

My friend Sunshine Daye always talks about 'the feeling tone' of things. Now you get to practise building your positive feeling muscles so that you can get busy pouring rocket fuel into your creations.

For each of the following sentences I invite you to close your eyes and tap into your emotions. Become aware of what you feel in each situation and deliberately try to increase feelings like joy, excitement, happiness, playfulness, compassion, gratitude, appreciation and love. I know that you have an amazing mind and you will easily be able to bring forth all kinds of positive feelings to support each of these scenes.

1. Imagine yourself on a really fancy, super-comfortable sun lounger on a golden, sandy beach. The weather is bright and sunny and the temperature is just perfect for you. If you prefer to lounge in the shade, imagine the perfect umbrella keeping the brightest sun off your body. Someone brings you your favourite drinks and it's all paid for.

2. You are getting ready to go on a date with the love of your life. You take time to get ready, you pick out your clothes with extra care and you imagine how perfect and wonderful the date will be.

3. You have been receiving treatment for a serious diagnosis for a long time and you have just been told by your specialist that you are healed.

4. You land your dream job, in the perfect location, earning 10k more than you thought you could get, with a comprehensive benefits package and full relocation expenses.

5. You win 100 million on the local lottery.

6. You visit an old church and have a profound mystical experience. Just for a moment you are aware that you are connected to everything and everyone in the entire universe.

Some of these are going to feel more real than others. I have deliberately given a range of experiences that happen to people. Remember these exercises are all about awareness, nothing more. And, as always, it's a practice.

You may want to write your experiences down in your journal to help you notice how you and your life are changing as you work through this book. Be okay with slowly embodying the principles and practices that we talk about. You are doing brilliantly, keep taking the inspired action and keep reading, there is so much more to know.

Chapter 7

UNDERSTANDING THE FIELDS AND THE WEEDS

"The world we are experiencing today is the result of our collective consciousness, and if we want a new world, each of us must start taking responsibility for helping create it."

~ ROSEMARY FILLMORE RHEA

Foundation 4

One Mind : My mind is one with the collective consciousness. I am at choice about where I place my mental attention, energy and focus.

Quantum science tells us that in it's smallest part everything in the universe is energy. We are all made up of the same energy, each expressing it as our unique selves. Some of us are more aware and sensitive to this energy than others. Some are almost oblivious on a conscious level, but as we saw earlier in the book, we are all transmitting and receiving that energy even if we don't directly sense it. There are an increasing number of highly sensitive people appearing on the planet who are constantly aware of the shifting emotional energy of other people and the planet as a whole. Highly sensitive people can easily fall into someone else's emotional or thought bucket. So it is important to understand a little more about this energy and how to cope with it when it's not what you want to experience. There is some good news. Even for the most sensitive among us, it's not a requirement to get stuck in other people's buckets and, the more aware you become, the easier it is to stop.

Going back to the HeartMath® information we looked at earlier - remember it said that our energy fields extend several feet beyond our bodies? It is possible that our personal energy field may project out for over a mile, but the scientists haven't yet found a way to measure this. If that were true, how many people do you think are within a mile radius of you right now? As I write this, I would think I have upwards of 20,000 people in my radius. We are all transmitting and receiving energetic information to and from each other, *constantly*.

Imagine all those people in your energy field. How might their thoughts and feelings be affecting your life and visa versa? Remember, unless you live alone on an island, you are constantly interacting with other people's energy, in the form of thoughts and emotions.

Every once in a while I spend time with someone who really drains my energy. They may not do it intentionally, in fact they may be oblivious, but I leave feeling exhausted. You may know someone like that yourself. I call them *energy vampires*. If spending time in the physical company of one person can drain your energy, imagine how you *could* be affected by the mass of people.

"The mass of men lead lives of quiet desperation."
~ HENRY DAVID THOREAU

If Thoreau is accurate with his assessment, you may be regularly tapping into those feelings of desperation as well as all the other vast array of human emotions. Whilst I believe we are rapidly moving towards a global shift in consciousness, into a time where humanity awakens to the truly spectacular and powerful creation that we are, there are still many people in our world who live in fear, lack and, as Thoreau says, *quiet desperation*. If that has been you then I'm glad you are reading this book. I got up from that place, and I know you can too.

Our individual minds and energies are connected to the collective mind and energy. Just as we can use our individual imaginations and emotions for a greater or lesser experience, that same energy is also going into the collective consciousness or unified field, as it's sometimes known, where it can create war, peace and every other type of experience.

We are all part of a collective *mind* field. Each of us is endlessly sharing our consciousness and our energy. Once I became aware of the power of my thoughts and feelings within the collective, I became far more intentional about what I focussed on. I don't want to be causing the *mind field* to become a *mine field* because of my careless thoughts. Don't panic though - fortunately this creative process doesn't happen the second you have a particular thought. It is through the constant repetition and the associated strong feeling that our thoughts start to solidify in the world.

The only influence you can have on the collective mind is through what *you* are projecting into it. Your thoughts and emotions are powerful. Every thought you think and emotion you experience is transmitted into the collective. As you start to change your thinking and believing, you have the power to change more than your own life, simply by being you. Your new choices about how you think, what you believe and the way you change your habits to reflect your new understanding will be noticed by many people in your life. When people start changing, becoming happier, achieving greater fulfillment and looking brighter, the people around them get curious and will want to learn more about what you are doing. Your gradual transformation will seem to others like a light has been switched on within you. Just remember, every great light will attract some bugs. Not everyone you meet will be delighted to share in your new discoveries. It is not your job to convert them, no matter how much your life is changing or how evangelical you may be. We are all on the perfect adventure in our own lives. We'll each come to an expanded personal experience in the right way and right time for us. No amount of encouragement or persuasion can get someone started who just isn't ready yet. Show up, shine your light and be ready to answer questions when they come. That's the best you can do.

The power of the collective mind

There have been many great demonstrations of proactively using the collective mind for good. In 1993 Dr. John Hagelin led a study with 4000 participants in Washington, DC. The volunteers came from Maharishi Mahesh Yogi's Transcendental Meditation and TM-Sidhi Programs. The aim of the experiment was to investigate what impact the collective mind could have on the crime rates in the area when a large group of trained people came together to meditate. The experiment took place through the months of June and July. Each day, for a specific period of time, the entire group would meditate together, practising the mindful process of Transcendental Meditation.

The population in the city at the time was about 1.5 million. A little under 4000 people meditating didn't seem like it would make a big difference. The team of researchers predicted a 20% drop in violent crime and the Chief of Police at the time said it would take a foot of snow in June to reduce crime by that amount. I'm sure that's one sound bite he wishes he could take back.

Everyone was surprised by the reductions that were experienced. Violent crime in the city gradually reduced as the meditating group grew in size. The final reduction in violent crime at the end of the experiment was 24%. However, based on the steady gain through the period of the test, it was predicted that a consistent group of 4000 people meditating in Washington, DC would create a lasting reduction in crime of 48%.

Research like this has been repeated in major cities and war zones all over the world with remarkably consistent findings. The collective mind is powerful and can have a positive or negative affect on the local population and the wider society.

Imagine, just for a moment, that this level of result could be achieved globally because you, and others like you, are becoming more conscious and more intentional about what you believe as well as the thoughts and habits you practise every day. I believe this new world is possible and I believe that each one of us who deliberately changes our thoughts, beliefs and behaviours is directly changing the world.

The collective mind field receives every kind of thought and emotion, both those that we see as positive and negative. If we are still in a predominantly *negative* home or work environment, we can sometimes find ourselves being dragged down by the collective energy. This kind of environment may also make it more difficult to change our minds and keep them changed. In an energy-draining situation it can also feel more challenging to make new choices. This is an opportunity to choose to become more persistent and consistent with our own practice to keep our energy high. That way we can avoid the energy vampires, or at least avoid the affects they can create. One of the ways I remind myself of my truth is by writing it down on sticky notes and putting them all around my home. When I first started doing my live radio show from my computer, I was very nervous, so I even had an arrow-shaped sticky note pointing at the microphone saying, "breathe".

There are lots of ways you can remind yourself about who you are and how you want to show up. You could even create some pictures with positive statements on them and have them come up on your computer's screensaver. Every thought and feeling, as well as affecting your personal atmosphere, is going into the collective field and shaping the global atmosphere. For me I think it's worth the practice to keep my energy where I want the world to be.

Great minds think alike

Actively using the principle of collective consciousness within your home, school or work environment can be incredibly powerful. Imagine that you have a project that a group wants to co-create, such as a holiday to a fancy destination, or a great set of exam results, or even the successful launch of a new product or service. You may want to get a group together and try this out.

Spend some time as a group getting clear on what you want to achieve. Then using your powerful imaginations, come together for twenty minutes every day to consciously daydream about the successful outcome of the project, no matter what it is. You have nothing to lose, so see if you can engage in this as an experiment. Remember to play with people who are willing to put any doubt to one side. You don't want someone throwing stones in your collective pond.

"No one can make you feel inferior without your consent."

~ ELEANOR ROOSEVELT

In the natural world there is a strange thing that happens when a group of lobsters get stuck in a lobster pot. If one of the lobsters should happen to discover the way out and start to climb through the hole, the remaining lobsters will try to climb over them to escape but in the process end up pulling them back in. You may occasionally experience similar behaviour to this with some of the people in your life. The experiences and stories that have created their belief systems may cause them to become very fearful as they observe you growing your life and claiming your greatest yet to be. If you experience this I invite you to see it as clear evidence for how well you are doing on your journey. Do your best to feel compassion for others who may still be stuck in the *guilt, blame, shame game*. The best you can do for them is keep shining your light and be ready with the answers when the questions come.

You are the only thinker in your mind, therefore *you* decide what story you make up about anyone you meet along the path of life. To me it makes sense to make up loving, compassionate stories because I have no idea what another person has experienced in his or her life. When I come across people who are really stuck in circles of addiction, violence or abuse, I ask myself "What kind of childhood could have created this adult?" I'm still making up a story, but at least it is one that fills my heart and enables me to be fully present to the underlying truth of wholeness that exists within us all.

> *"Man's mind once stretched by a new idea, never*
> *regains its original dimension."*
>
> ~ OLIVER WENDELL HOLMES

When we have learned something new it cannot be easily forgotten. It is lodged in the recesses of our subconscious mind forever. Now you have opened your mind to a new perspective you will find yourself becoming more and more aware of the impact of this knowledge.

One such area of impact is health and the human body. As we think about the collective mind field across the planet, we become aware that there are so many different beliefs about health, healing, and the bodies ability to heal itself. Depending on where you are in the world, your beliefs will be impacted differently by the collective beliefs on this subject.

What do you believe about your physical body, its problems, the causes of those problems, and the body's ability to heal?

Your answer will, most likely, depend on where and when you

were born. Take a moment to answer this question right now. We'll be checking back to see if it's possible for you to change your mind in a few short pages.

Facts are opinions based on current knowledge

In the 1950s smoking was considered to have health benefits. Even earlier in history blood-letting, the practice of cutting open the body and allowing it to bleed freely, used to be considered a viable treatment for a number of diseases, as was the use of leeches. We have a different opinion about the efficacy of these practices today. Through time almost everything we think we know can change. Here is another great example of this type of change: I recently watched a TED talk with Kelly McGonigal, who proposed that stress, today's biggest underlying cause of disease, is not fundamentally good or bad. Your body responds to stress based on what you believe about it. Ms. McGonigal has undertaken academic research about what happens in our bodies under stress, then looked at how this changes when the mind has been reprogrammed to believe the body's stress response is 'normal'. She finally extrapolated that: When it come to stress, "it is done unto us as we believe". Perhaps you have read that somewhere recently. This is one more demonstration that there are no real 'facts', there is only the current level of understanding and knowledge.

Over the centuries, as humanity has increased its use of technology, we have learned more and more about what is healthy and what isn't. The paradox to this is the wisdom held in some of the most remote and so called "primitive" tribes around our globe. There are a number of remote tribes of people, each of which has its own civilisation and culture, who have not been impacted by our technology and where very few people in the tribe ever get sick. Should there be any kind of disease or injury, they are not airlifted to the nearest hospital, but rather are successfully treated with herbs, prayer and magic or mental/spiritual healing from those in the community trained in such things. Not everyone will heal, but most do.

So where does that leave us? In some studies, modern science is meeting up with ancient wisdom, reminding us that our bodies have the ability to self-heal *if* they are in a healthy environment. Dr Bernie Siegel has been working in the field of cancer recovery for many years and has written a host of books on the subject. In each of his books he has reported several cases of, what he calls, *exceptional patients,* who have completely healed when medical science didn't have a cure, or had predicted a very short life expectancy. A friend of mine was diagnosed with lung cancer and given six months to live. He went on to live a busy and thriving life for over five years.

You can change your mind

There are many stories of so called 'miracle' healings. These stories may include different complementary therapies, energy healers, hypnotherapy, visualisation, prayer, and dietary changes. Generally, allopathic medicine does not have answers as to why these healings may have taken place. One of the most fascinating pieces of research that specifically addresses changing the mind involves people experiencing multiple personality disorders. This information further affirms my belief in the idea that changing your thoughts and beliefs can change your physical experience, and even your physical body. In people diagnosed with multiple personality disorder, one of the personalities may need glasses, yet with a change of character, another personality may have 20:20 vision. That change happens with no time delay, the change is instant - as the mind changes, so does the vision.

In one case, reported by Dr. Bennet Braun, a psychiatrist at Rush-Presbyterian-St. Luke's Medical Center in Chicago, in an individual with many personalities, one personality drinks orange juice with no ill affects. If any of the other personalities within the individual drink orange juice, they get hives. Even if the orange-juice-safe personality leaves whilst the orange juice is still being digested, the hives kick in. Even more remarkably, as soon as the original orange-juice-safe personality comes back in to control the body, the hives immediately stop itching and the blisters begin to rapidly subside.

This type of report, and there are many, further convince me of the power of the mind, as well as the body-mind connection. There has been a tendency in traditional Western medicine to hold true to the Descartes belief that the mind and body are separate things. This view is starting to diminish as we learn so much more about consciousness, the anatomy of the brain, cell biology and quantum physics. To me, the examples from people experiencing multiple personality disorder are compelling evidence of the *total human*. Think back to the idea that each of your trillions of cells is behaving like an ant in a colony. You cannot be separated into parts. Humans are not like a clock, we cannot be disassembled into all our functional parts, put back together again, wound up and be back in working order. We are much more complicated than that.

> *"The most powerful tool in the doctor's 'little black bag' to prevent or treat illness is the patient's (your) own mind!"*
> ~ BERNIE SIEGEL

In her classic book *You Can Heal Your Life*, Louise Hay offers a long list of 'wrong thinking' that may be the cause of physical disease. Ms. Hay healed herself from cancer through practising what she teaches. Dr. Bernie Siegal reports on years of working with patients experiencing cancer who have been able to heal themselves without surgery, through the use of creative visualisation and other whole body techniques.

Our beliefs and feelings can be just as powerful in creating healing in our bodies as they can in creating parking spaces and green traffic lights. There is no limit to what we can create from our mind, other than what we believe. Now is the time to think a little deeper.

I asked you this question earlier:

"What do you believe about your physical body, its problems, the causes of those problems, and its ability to heal?"

In a couple of short pages, have you changed your mind about what's possible?

Again, there is no right or wrong in the answer to this question. You may want to dive deeper into why you believe what you believe and check in with how that belief is supporting you. Remember our story about young Joe. Is it possible that you are clinging to a belief simply because it has never been reprogrammed?

How different could the world be if we all opened our minds to a greater possibility of healing and wholeness? If you are seeking to ignite success beyond beliefs in the area of physical healing I invite you to spend a little more time thinking about your beliefs in this area. Pay particular attention to investigating what you believe about western medicine, complementary medicine and faith/spiritual healing. You may discover that some of your beliefs may be keeping you stuck.

This in no way suggests that Western allopathic medicine is bad or not useful. There is a place for everything and everyone in our global family. It is the recognition that there is more to know (true in every aspect of life), about the potential for human health and well-being. As we, individually, awaken to our own potential and change our minds about our ability to heal, we automatically transmit this expanded awareness into the collective field and, by the very nature of energy, that information is received by all of us. When we reach the critical mass (the amount needed to tip the see-saw), we can change physical outcomes, as did the 4000 meditators in Washington, DC.

Every garden will always have some weeds.

There are somewhere over seven billion people on the planet and we're all transmitting our thoughts, feelings and beliefs into the collective mind field. Just like that one person who can drain your energy, some of what is getting transmitted into the field isn't in alignment with what *you* want to experience. That is why we still see such an amazing diversity of experience all over the globe.

In recognition that we are all at choice and we are all constantly transmitting our consciousness and beliefs into the collective mind, it is good to remember that we don't have to share our physical time with those who energetically drain us and don't support us. I have found that this often happens very organically. Gradually you have less and less in common and you drift apart. This is more difficult if those people are members of your family, or people you want to stay in relationship with. In that case one of the best things to do is not to fall into their bucket. Don't engage in conversations about how difficult life is. Remember that we are all divine sparks doing the best we can. Writing this reminds me of a story I heard. I don't fully remember the details but it was about a teacher of this philosophy, someone who had trained as a counsellor in the Science of Mind and Spirit. When he had clients come to him telling him how dreadful everything was, he would keep repeating in his mind that they were simply trying to trick him, that he really knew that they were divine spark, that he would not be fooled by their 'story' of challenge, lack, sickness or limitation. Perhaps you can try remembering that when you are faced with people who are not yet ready to look at their beliefs.

I would suggest you don't try to 'correct' them or preach to them. Each one of us has to come to these ideas in the perfect moment for us. And until we are ready, having someone tell us we are wrong is just annoying. Your life will be the demonstration, and as people get curious about how you seem to be happier, more peaceful and more compassionate, they will want to know what you're up to. Then you get to evangelise.

Where do you put your attention?

Several years ago I made a very conscious and intentional decision to release TV and newspapers from my life. It was easy for me, I didn't have any teenagers in the house. I have been delighted at how I always know about any significant events that are happening in the world even though I don't watch, listen or read any news programs. It's not that I am taking an ostrich-like approach to world events. I am simply not *choosing* to put my attention, energy and focus into them. By falling into the bucket of fear, lack, despair, hatred, jealousy, anger, judgement, doubt and separation, which the media tends to create, I end up feeling yucky inside. Instead I choose to make my own well-being my highest priority and stay clear of that kind of reporting. Now when I get to hear about difficult world events, the information comes as a matter of fact, rather than an emotive report from media trying to increase their viewer ratings. When I'm not bombarded by other people's emotions and beliefs I am better able to stay centred and do what I do best, which is to apply my spiritual practice to remind myself of a higher truth.

You are always at choice even if your choice is to tune into the news, in whatever form. It may serve you well to remember that you are reading or listening to information which is processed through the filters of other people's thoughts, emotions and beliefs. Those filters may have created a very different *truth*. You get to weed your garden, both internally and externally. Just because you were raised to do certain things, in certain ways, doesn't mean you have to keep doing them if they no longer serve the path you wish to travel. Not only *can* you change your mind, but if you want to experience a new reality, it's inevitable that you will.

There may be times when you experience events or situations happening in the world, locally or globally, that you don't want to see. Remember what you have learned in this book. Recognise that you are not holding those kinds of thoughts in your mind and yet they are being created. Rather than worry about what might be happening in your mind, remember that over seven billion others are sending their thoughts into the collective mind, and each one gets to choose the 'movie' they are watching.

Your only responsibility is to yourself, to enable you to be as peaceful, joyous and loving as you can. The more mental time you are able to spend in that 'happy' place and the less time you spend in drama, lack and fear, the better your life will work and the more evidence you will see that you are igniting success beyond beliefs.

Chapter 7 Awareness Exercise - Practise Weeding

With around 75,000 thoughts a day, you are going to have some thoughts that are not creating the kind of spectacular life that you really want, or that you want to be projecting into the collective mind. Catching those thoughts gets easier the more you practise.

It is important to remember that the work in this exercise is not an excuse to become critical or judgemental of yourself or others. It is an awareness practice to help you clean up your mental chatter.

Affirm for yourself, "It gets easier and easier for me to weed my mental garden and choose thoughts that nourish and support me."

In my experience, it is sometimes more difficult to catch yourself when you are in the heat of the moment. So for this exercise, to help you become more present with how you think and what the 'chatter' says in your mind, I invite you to think about your day yesterday and answer these questions.

1. What situations caused your mind to fall into guilt, shame, blame, judgement, fear, irritation, anger or any other *negative* thoughts?

2. When you fell into the bucket of negative thoughts, what feelings and sensations did you experience in your physical body?

3. For each occasion in question 1, how could you deliberately replay that experience with more supportive and empowering thoughts?

4. When you replay the *positive* thoughts, what feelings and sensations do you experience in your body?

Now take the *positive* feelings that you experience and imagine spreading them through your body with every breath you breathe. Imagine those good feelings breathing into every cell and every particle of your body. As you practise this, you are re-wiring your brain to expect to embody more of these good feelings. This change causes your brain to *look* for more good thoughts so you can embrace the good feelings, and this is how you retrain the brain to get better and better at catching yourself when you mentally go off on a rampage of unsupportive thinking. Just like everything in life, it's a practice, and I promise it gets easier.

Chapter 8

HOW DOES YOUR GARDEN GROW?

*"And the day came when the risk to
remain tight in a bud was more painful
than the risk it took to blossom."*

~ ANAÏS NIN

Foundation 5

**3Ps : There are many ways to re-wire the mind.
Practise, Persistence and Patience are required in any
construction project and I am always under
construction.**

The 3Ps of Practise, Persistence and Patience are a cornerstone of my teaching. Over and over in my life I have proved to myself that experiences I desire can be achieved through the application of these 3Ps. Now I want to pass that baton to you and invite you to create new habits of persistent practise whilst remaining patient with the worldly results.

As a young child you already mastered the 3Ps. You learned to walk. You fell down over and over. You had no evidence that you could walk, but you could see others doing it. Somewhere within you was an impulse, a desire, that could not be ignored. So you kept practising, you showed great persistence, there may have been times when you went back to crawling, but you didn't make up a story saying, "I'm not destined to walk." You just kept at it. With Practise, Persistence and Patience one day you were able to walk. Sometimes you fell over, or got a bit wobbly, but you still kept up your practise. You probably don't often think about your ability to walk these days. And you probably don't fall over very often. You are now a master of walking. Are you ready to be a master of your mind?

"Life is a journey, not a destination."
~ RALPH WALDO EMERSON

It's 'True Confessions' time. I sometimes struggle with the third 'P' - Patience. I can occasionally be just a little impatient. I have even been known to throw a two-year-old-style tantrum and metaphorically stamp my feet when things have not worked in my timescale or not gone quite how I was wanting or expecting them to go. Has that ever happened to you?

Even though I still have these occasional moments of forgetfulness, I have learned there is something truly awesome about the way the Universe delivers my good when I *practise persistently*. Remember, the only thing that is limiting the delivery of that good is what you believe about what you can receive. There is not some heavenly host observing your every move, judging your behaviour, and deciding what you can or cannot have. The Infinite Intelligence that is Life brings unseen waves of energy from nothing into something for you to receive what you desire. Depending on what you are calling forth into creation, and how long you have been experiencing the absence of that thing, it can take time to appear in the physical world. The key is to stick with the 3Ps.

One of the first things to practise is being okay with who and where you are right now.

Earlier in the book I mentioned that judgement and criticism don't motivate change. I also spoke to the idea that you are already perfect (within your human imperfection). This is an excellent place to remind you about these things.

Sometimes, in our urgency to rush into our next *greatest yet to be,* we forget that we are already here. We spend all our mental time, and energy, re-scripting the past and worrying about the future. We forget that the impulsion calling us forward into new growth is a result of everything we have already experienced and all that we currently are. Self-acceptance and self-compassion are both practises vitally important to your ongoing sense of wellbeing. They allow a platform of nurture, rather than criticism, to be the base for new growth.

When I Loved Myself Enough is a little book by Kim and Alison McMillen. Every page completes a 'When I loved myself enough' statement. For example, *When I loved myself enough I redefined success and life became simple. Oh, the pleasure of that.* This inspiring little book - it's only about four inches (ten centimetres) square - lives on a table in my sitting room and is always within arm's reach when I need to remember to love myself. You may have other things you use to remind you. It matters not what you do, but that you practise loving all that you are, or at least, being willing to love and accept all that you are. The more persistent you are with your practise the sooner you will start to feel better about everything in life.

I did not find it easy to move into a place of true self love. Even now, after many years of diligent practise, my inner critic goes on the occasional rampage. That opens the door for our next practise - forgiveness.

"Forgiveness is not an occasional act, it is a constant attitude."
~ Martin Luther King Jr.

Let's get one thing clear right away. Forgiveness has got absolutely nothing to do with any other person. Forgiveness is about setting yourself free from the pain of something that hurt you in the past. That past could be moments ago, and it could be decades. If you are still living your days clinging to an old story about how someone did you wrong and how they need to apologise or make amends for their behaviour, you are creating your very own bed of nails and sleeping there every day.

Imagine that one day a friend shared some food with you and you had an unexpected allergic reaction to it. It was unfortunate, but these things happen. Your friend sends her apologies and a Get Well Soon card and goes about her business. When you stay stuck in un-forgiveness, it's like feeding *yourself* that same food, getting sick all over again and blaming your friend. She doesn't even know what you are doing, you are the only one suffering.

This may seem like a flippant example. I have worked with people who have experienced incredibly challenging events in their lives including rape, incest, physical and mental abuse, and many other things. I fully understand how hard it can be to move into forgiveness. However the result is the same. When you stay stuck in any past trauma, no matter how large or small, you are the only person suffering.

Here's another story, which illustrates this idea really well.

There was once a slightly unruly child who had spent some of her very early life living in a children's home before being adopted into a traditional family. At thirteen years old she was a typical teenager, pushing boundaries, testing the possibilities and thinking she knew everything. One day, like many of the days at that point in her life, she got into a heated argument with her dad. The poor man was frustrated that his daughter would not do what he wanted her to do, whilst the daughter was equally frustrated because no one seemed to be able to hear what she was saying. As the row escalated, her dad spoke these words, "If you don't tow the line I'm going to have you put back in a children's home."

To the young girl these words were like a knife to the heart. They confirmed her already-held belief that she was no good, unlovable and unwanted. These words hardened like stones around her heart. As she grew, she would mentally take them out and polish them, each time remembering all the pain of that fight, building the anger, frustration and bitterness towards her father, re-enforcing the beliefs in her worthlessness and inability to be loved. Anytime she felt wounded she would go back to that memory and once again live it, feel it, and grow the feelings and beliefs. Her heart became harder and harder.

One day, many years later, someone talked to the girl, who was now a woman, about forgiveness. "I could never forgive this," she said. But, as she re-told the story, one she had repeated so many times, tears started to roll down her face. Something opened within her just the tiniest bit, one of the stones around her heart crumbled a little, and willingness sneaked in.

The woman started to learn more and more about her mind, about life and about forgiveness. She did many exercises, released lots of stuck emotion and slowly began forgiving things she had carried for so very long. There were many stones around her heart, they had formed great layers, each had to be chipped gently away, one at a time. Inevitably she came to the last layer. 'That story' was all that was left to release. Gradually, even that melted away and she felt free for the first time in almost twenty-five years.

Eventually she plucked up the courage to speak to her dad about that event, which had had such a significant and lasting impact on the first half of her adult life. When she told him the story and asked him why he had said such a terrible thing, he looked at her blankly and said he didn't remember ever having said those words. And even if he had, he hadn't meant it.

Getting past the idea that forgiveness is about anyone other than you is the first step. The second step is *willingness*. Right where you are, you may have no clue how you could possibly forgive whomever or whatever you choose to forgive. That's okay. All that you need is willingness. Open a space within yourself to be willing to forgive the person, people or situation, no matter how far away that might feel or how impossible you think it is. Moving to willingness is a massive step from "No" to "Maybe." That is a quantum leap in forgiveness terms. I know this because I was that *slightly unruly child*. I was blessed to be able to resolve the feelings I carried about my father and to set myself free through this experience. I now see it as a great teaching tool for forgiveness.

Because we are energy, operating in more energy, something about *willingness* opens an energetic space in the Universe which allows things to start moving. You don't have to know how, just be willing to forgive, be willing to love and accept yourself, be willing to ignite success in your life, and keep moving forward.

The power of your word

> *"Think twice before you speak, because your words and*
> *influence will plant the seed of either success or failure*
> *in the mind of another."*
>
> NAPOLEON HILL

Perhaps you have never contemplated just how powerful words are. For a moment, right now, take a breath. Consider the last words that you spoke in anger to someone else. As you recall that moment, how did you feel? Taking another deep breath, bring to mind the last words you spoke with love to someone. How did you feel when you spoke words of love?

Every word we speak has immense power. Every sound and syllable has its own vibration. Every word has a meaning upon which the collective mind has agreed. That meaning has a vibration or an energy signal just like the broadcast signals that come forth from the TV and radio transmitters. If you want to see the pattern for a word you speak, record your voice into any software that shows the sound pattern. If you are a Mac user then you have something called GarageBand that comes on your computer. I use this all the time to record my meditations and podcasts. I find it quite fascinating that every word I speak has its own visual pattern. After all this time I can *see* certain words without listening to them when I look at the sound track because I know what they look like.

Just like the local radio station, you are broadcasting your words hither and thither. How much thought do you put into them before you set them free?

I know in my own life there have been many occasions when I have engaged my mouth long before my brain has caught up. Consequently there have been many occasions when I have made a fool of myself or I have hurt or offended others. All because I was thoughtless in the use of my powerful words.

When we wake up to the power of our words we can radically change how we use them. Rather than being mind*less*, we can become mind*ful* with our words. We can intentionally and deliberately create words and sentences in such a way that they empower us, support change, uplift others and make a difference in the lives of millions. One such way of using words is in affirmations. I have mentioned affirmations a couple of times already and I have used examples of them; "*I am willing to change*" is one such example.

Affirmations are positive statements that are made in the first person and the present moment. For example: I am vibrantly healthy; I now live in the constant flow of infinite opulence; I have every resource I need to ignite my success and live my dream life. You get the idea.

There are some basic principles when it comes to using affirmations affectively.

1. Always use "I" or "We" when stating your good. Claiming or declaring something in this way is amazingly powerful. "I Am" statements have a power all their own. That which you place "I am" before, you tend to become.

2. Be here, now. Universal energy has no concept of time and space. There is only *now*. If you start saying "I will" or "I am going to" you are putting things into the future, and as the song says, "tomorrow never comes."

3. Only use *confirming* statements, the Universe doesn't understand negative or refuting statements. Using the power of your word in affirmations is a bit like animal communication. When you *speak* to your animal you are sending images, when you say, "don't chew the door", your animal sees a picture of chewing the door so thinks that's okay. When you say "I am not fat", "I am not broke", or "I am no longer sick", guess what mental pictures are being created in the Collective Mind?

4. Everything you say is an affirmation. Every word that forms in your mind and is then uttered out into the world is an affirmation. Every word goes forth into the world and has the power to uplift, support, engage and embrace, or the power to crush, destroy, isolate or reject. On some level every word is creating something. The only person that allows those pearls of wisdom to fall from your mouth is you. What will you choose?

In Step 1 I said, "'I Am' statements have a power all their own. That which you place 'I am' before, you tend to become." I want to dive a little deeper into this concept. Try these statements out:

- I am sick
- I am angry

- I am stupid
- I am worthless

How do they feel in your body? What sense do you get from the above statements? And how often have you said some or all of them? Now try these 'antidotes'; the reversal of the first set of statements.

- I am vibrantly healthy
- I am peaceful
- I am amazingly intelligent
- I am worthy and deserving

Do you feel the difference? When you use, "I am" you are invoking the indwelling presence of divine energy. That is what I mean when I say, "That which you place 'I am' before, you tend to become." Try it out for yourself. Use this list or make up your own empowering 'I am' statements.

Using affirmations deliberately and very consciously is a powerful practise. Once you become clear about what you want to create in your life and how you want to experience life every day, then you can create affirmations to support the outcome. It may be that you can speak an affirmation once and receive the result immediately. More often, affirmations need repeating many times over. The repetition isn't for the Infinite Intelligence, it's for you and your belief system. Imagine being in a body that has been diagnosed with an illness that Western medicine says is "incurable". To be saying an affirmation something like, "I have a fit, healthy body that is thriving and alive in every cell" may feel like it's totally untrue. In that situation you find your inner voice saying, "Yeah, right, you need a reality check, didn't you hear what the doctor said?" Every word is an affirmation, even those that don't have the substance of a spoken vibration, which is why it is important that you create affirmations that *feel* true, on some level.

In our example above, adding some *willingness* into the

affirmation could make all the difference: "I am *willing* to have a fit, healthy body that is thriving and alive in every cell", this is immediately true for all of us. Now the chattering voice in your head cannot disagree, and you are in harmony with your affirmation. Once you achieve a harmony within yourself for the affirmations you are speaking they become powerful tools. It's like having a resonant frequency in a tuning fork. If you have a bunch of tuning forks in a space together and you strike one, the others that are the same frequency will start to vibrate in harmony. That's what happens to you when you are in harmony with your affirmations and that is when they become truly powerful.

The intention of affirmations is to change your mind, not to call forth something from the Infinite. We repeat affirmations so that they change what we believe is possible within us. Even the affirmations that don't feel miles away from truth, may still feel somewhat uncomfortable. That's why we repeat them. The human mind is one of habit. We repeat and repeat our affirmations until we can truly embody and believe them.

You are constantly changing and growing. Your affirmations need to change and grow with you.

You may spend some time getting really clear about what you want to experience. You craft an eloquent collection of affirmations and relish the experience of speaking them out into the world every day. But one day, you get started with them and they don't feel the same. Don't keep repeating them once the *feeling* changes. It means you have changed and it's time for some fresh sculpting of words to create new harmonious affirmations that support your ever-expanding self.

Equally, it's no good spending half a day getting clear, and birthing a set of powerful and supportive affirmations, and then never speaking them out. The whole point of affirmations is that they get spoken into the world. There is something remarkable about the power of the spoken word to create physical experience. It's not magic, it's science, but it is still something that I have respect and awe for because I don't fully understand everything that is at work within this law. I have the same degree of respect for electricity because it too can be harnessed for something truly magnificent, such as a life support machine, or something deadly like an electric chair. Your words are equally powerful, whether you are using them on yourself or others. Making time, every day, to speak your affirmations and to be in a place of harmony with them in your body is a powerful practise which also needs the other two Ps of Persistence and Patience.

> *"The key to growth is the introduction of higher*
> *dimensions of consciousness into our awareness."*
>
> ~ LAO TZU

The garden of our life and our consciousness, just like the physical garden, has to grow. It is a Law of Life. Take any bare patch of ground and within a few short weeks there are green and brown things sprouting through the soil, even when it looks like nothing could grow. You are no different. In every moment of your life cells in your body are dying and new cells are being created. In every breath you breathe your body is releasing toxins and bringing in nourishment in the form of oxygen. You can't help yourself, for as long as you are breathing, you are growing and changing. You have the power within you to shape some of that growth and change through your thoughts, words, feelings and beliefs. Mastering these tools takes Practise, Persistence & Patience. My invitation is that you keep doing all three Ps and you then become like the eager gardener in spring, watching for the new shoots to break through the soil and grasp the light.

Igniting success beyond beliefs takes all of our 5 foundations to be in balance and harmony. If these concepts are new to you, give yourself some time to play with them and experiment. You will be far better motivated to keep up the 3Ps if you have already gathered a body of evidence from the other foundations. Above all, be gentle with yourself. Be willing to go as slow as you feel you need to go. Life is a journey, remember, not a destination.

Chapter 8 Awareness Exercise - Seeding and Weeding

Planting new seeds into our mind is a very deliberate practise. Once those seeds are planted, we need to keep tending the soil of our consciousness by plucking out the weeds. On our journey of growth and change, weeds are thoughts that no longer serve us, people that don't support us and situations that drain our energy. As always, this exercise is about awareness. It is your opportunity to apply the 3Ps of Practise, Persistence and Patience in your own experience.

Step 1 - Planting seeds of self-acceptance

Here are three affirmations I invite you to speak out every day to help you plant the seeds of self-acceptance, self-compassion and self love. Repeat each one seven times in the morning and seven times in the evening for at least two weeks.

I am always doing the very best I can and I gently forgive myself when I think otherwise.

I am constantly in the process of growing and changing but my inner light always burns brightly and can never be diminished.

There is a spark within me that is always perfectly guided and going in the best direction. Every day I practise trusting, accepting and loving myself a little bit more, exactly as I am.

If any of these affirmations feel too far away from where you are right now, remember to bring a little *willingness* into the sentence. As an example, the first sentence could become:

I am willing to believe I am always doing the very best I can and I am willing to gently forgive myself when I think otherwise.

Step 2 - Plucking the weeds of resistance

Remember I mentioned the Borg alien race from StarTrek earlier in the book? Their catch phrase was "Resistance is futile". Never was a truer word spoken when it comes to the power of your mind to rewire and your consciousness to expand. Yet we still have to weed the garden like good gardeners.

The second part of this exercise is becoming the observer of your thoughts and picking out the unsupportive or outdated ones when they pop up.

As you say the affirmations above out loud, be very mindful about the chattering voice in your head. Once you have gone through saying all the affirmation seven times, take your journal or note pad and write down anything that is coming up from the chattering voice of your inner critic. Try not to get into an argumentative dialogue; become like the impartial observer in an exam room. It is not your role to have an opinion. You are there to watch and observe and notice what is happening.

As you jot down anything that comes to your awareness, take a moment to think about where it may have come from and then ask yourself these questions:

- Is it still true for me?
- Is it something that was planted by someone else's belief system?
- Am I ready to weed this thought?

If you are ready to weed the thought, use your imagination to pluck it out of your mind and put it in the rubbish or the compost bin. If you are not ready to weed it, be okay with that. Everything comes in its perfect time.

When a negative thought continually pops up, come up with a new affirmation that will neutralise it. Here's an example:

You say the affirmation, "I am always doing the very best I can and I gently forgive myself when I think otherwise."

The negative thought comes up, "No you're not, just look at how rude you were to that driver who cut you off the other day. If that's your best, you're in big trouble."

The neutralising affirmation could be something like this, "I forgive myself for reacting in a moment of forgetfulness. I know that I am in the process of change and I am choosing to be gentle with myself through the journey. I remember I am always doing the best I can, even when it doesn't look too pretty."

The more you practise the easier it gets. Remember to be gentle with yourself.

How Does Your Garden Grow?

Chapter 9

NOURISHING YOUR SUITCASE

*"If I don't look after my body, I'll
have nowhere to live."*

~ 87 YEAR YOUNG HOMELESS MAN

You may have heard that your body is a temple. I'm sure that is
true on some level. Personally, I prefer to think of the body as a
Suitcase. In my mind, my body is a transportation or carrying device
for the part of me that is more than carbon atoms. The part which
some traditions call Spirit, Soul or Source. I believe my body is a
device for Source Energy within me to experience Life through me.
To my mind that makes my body really important; in fact it makes it
essential for this experience. In this chapter we will be investigating
how to ignite success beyond beliefs when it comes to health and
well-being. How is your suitcase doing? How do you nourish your
body?

Just as there is a vast array of bags and cases in the world, the
diversity of humans is no different. Similarly, we don't know the
contents of any suitcase until we look inside.

The opening quote comes from a story told by Jason 'Juice
Master' Vale in a video clip I watched. An 87-years-young homeless
man was interviewed for a TV program in Ireland. He had lived on
the streets for a significant amount of time with no home and no job,
and yet he was really fit and well. In fact he was far healthier than

anyone would have expected for a man of his age living rough. When asked by the interviewer what his secret was he replied, "Firstly, living on the streets is a choice for me, as I like the freedom that it affords me." He went on to explain that he also didn't eat "junk food", but that he would be given left over fruit and veg by the market stall holders at the end of every day, which, as he didn't have any means to cook, he would eat raw. He also received the occasional healthy meal provided by local restaurants, as he was well known and liked in the local community. He went on to say that he was very fussy about what he put into his body, finally closing with this, "You see, the reason I don't eat junk food is because if I don't look after my body, I'll have nowhere to live."

Perhaps you may have seen this man on the streets and made up a story about his health or well-being. At the same time, how often do we read about some young, apparently fit and healthy person, dropping dead from a heart attack or aneurism? We don't know what's on the inside until we take a look. When did you last take an inventory of what is happening inside your suitcase? When was the last time you reviewed how you are nourishing your body? Thinking about food, drink, rest, exercise, play and inspiration, how conscious are you of looking after your physical suitcase, and are you doing what you can to ensure you have somewhere to live into your 80s or 90s? Personally I fancy living until I'm at least 106; how long do you think your body will last if you keep treating it the way you do now?

"It is never too late to be what you might have been."

~ GEORGE ELIOT

The human body is a radiant example of Ms. Eliot's quote. No matter how you may have failed to nourish your body thus far in your life, it has an in-built healing ability which, when you change your beliefs and behaviour, you can harness. I have proven this to myself in recent years by going from being a confirmed "junk food" addict to being someone who eats a far healthier diet consisting largely of plant-based whole foods. For people who knew me well, my decision to make this change was something of a surprise to them, but for me it was a natural result of changing my life from the inside out. I came to recognise that the way I was nourishing my physical body was totally out of alignment with everything else I practised and believed. For me it was the last area of my life where I needed to change my beliefs. For many people it is one of the first areas they come to.

Reverend Michael Bernard Beckwith says, *"the pain pushes until the vision pulls."* That is exactly what happened with my change of mind concerning my body. I started to have some aches and pains, some minor problems that I'd never had before, and I started to worry that there may be something more challenging building beneath the surface. I don't usually choose to use mainstream allopathic medicine so started to do some research into other options. I found a great movie called "Forks Over Knives" which looks at how you can eat differently and thereby create well-being and vibrant health in your body. That first film led me down a rabbit hole of similar and related films, and I also read the data research that the films referred to.

Having completed so much research, I realised that although I spent lots of time developing and cleansing my emotional, mental and spiritual health, I spent almost no time on my physical health. I was out of alignment with my belief system. I recognised that neglecting my physical suitcase was, on a subconscious level, an act of self-sabotage, not an act of self-love. So I made the change and stepped into a whole new way of nourishing my body. Do I still eat the occasional doughnut? Hell yes! But when I do, I am present and conscious and I do it with love.

Trust your body, it knows

At the beginning of this book we discussed the concept that *you* get to define success in your life. I also said that fundamentally you can never be anything other than successful because you are here and breathing, you are a living embodiment of the success principle. With all that said, how successful do you feel when you are struggling with colds, viruses, aches and pains? Where are you on the success chart when you constantly feel tired and mentally foggy? These symptoms may indicate that you are not nourishing your body suitcase in a way that serves you. You are not balancing vibrant, life-giving food and drink with exercise and play that is fun, and rest that renews and revitalises you on every level. We have all heard about balancing "work, rest and play", but are you practising these things equally in your life?

When you change your habits, your life experience will be different. I may have mentioned previously that I can be a bit impatient and I have also been known to be a little stubborn occasionally. As I started to learn more about the leading edge ideas on nutrition, well-being, health and the human body, I realised that if I were going to change my habits I would have to do something significant. I did lots of research, my own version of 'due diligence', about the pros and cons of juicing, the build up of toxins in the body, how the cells receive the nutrients from the digestive system, and many other areas of study that were new to me. As well as *Forks Over Knives*, I watched movies such as: *Food Matters; Crazy Sexy Cancer; Fat, Sick And Nearly Dead* and I read a number of books about food, nutrition and the body. As a result of all this research I decided that my 'something significant' would be a seven day juice detox led by Jason Vale.

That was my kick start into nourishing my body suitcase in a way it had probably never experienced before. It is not the only way, it is simply what called to me. Juicing and smoothies continue to be a significant part of my nutritional program, but the most important thing that has happened through this process is that I am now incredibly conscious about what I eat. That doesn't mean that I never eat nutritionally poor food, it means that I do it consciously and ensure that I balance the choices I make, so that 80% of the time I am in alignment with great nutrition. The results within my body astounded me. I had even more energy, faster mental processing, clearer skin, needed less sleep and, as a side affect, I lost around three stone (42 pounds or 19 kilos) in weight.

I hope my story inspires you. Perhaps you are not ready for seven days of juicing and smoothies, but when did you last take time out to look at your diet, think about the liquids you drink, and consider how you are nourishing your body? If you want to ignite greater success in your physical body, changing your mind about how and what you eat could make all the difference.

Getting yourself on a conscious nutritional program, which suits your body and works for your lifestyle, is the first step to physical vibrancy.

The illustrations below demonstrate the value of getting all elements of your physical well-being in alignment. It doesn't matter in which order you decide to work on these areas. You may already be great at resting your body or taking time out to play. Start with the area that makes you most uncomfortable, because when you make changes and see the results, you'll feel better about yourself and be more motivated to make further changes.

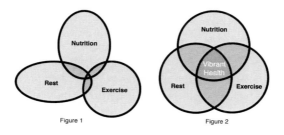

Figure 1   Figure 2

In Figure 1 above there is very little opportunity for a vibrantly healthy life when nutrition, rest and exercise are not in balance. Conversely, in Figure 2, we see how different things can be when we become conscious of our physical life.

"Take rest; a field that has rested gives a bountiful crop."

~ Ovid

I am regularly baffled by the number of people who seem to believe that rest is a bad thing. Personally I think we would all be better served to take our lead from puppies (pardon the pun), who will eat and play and chase and play and eat and then fall over, be in a deep sleep until they are fully rested, then the fun starts again. What are your beliefs about rest? Do you get all the sleep, relaxation and play that your body needs to maintain vibrant health?

A friend of mine always says she can't sleep during the day, no matter how tired she is. I happen to know that is a belief programmed by her father. I was never encouraged to sleep during the day unless I was sick, in which case I wasn't allowed out of bed. That could have set up some programming for me, but I joined the Navy and ended up working crazy long shifts for a few months. I soon mastered the art of sleeping and resting at every opportunity, a skill that has remained part of my life to this day.

I have very deliberately put *sleep* and *relaxation* as two separate things on this list because we can relax deeply without falling asleep *and* we can be asleep without relaxing. Have you ever woken from a long night of sleep but felt completely un-rested? I know I have. That's why incorporating relaxation practices into your daily life is so valuable.

One way to relax your body very deliberately is to breathe deeply and with great awareness. Dr. Andrew Weill says, "Diet and exercise not withstanding, if I could only prescribe one thing to every patient I see, it would be 10 minutes of daily conscious breathing."

When we think of nourishment, breathing is the one thing we do constantly that both nourishes and revitalises our body. Conscious breathing, that is to bring your full awareness to your breath within your body, is a powerful practice that has multiple health benefits. When it comes to relaxation, I think it's a great place to start, because everyone breathes. How are you breathing right now?

Everyday life can get very hectic and we can become very lost in the events and drama. Although our subconscious mind keeps our body breathing, it often becomes very shallow as we become more tense. In extreme moments of stress, we stop breathing. Anyone who has experienced sleep apnoea will know how tiring it is to not get the amount of oxygen the body needs. Taking time out to sit comfortably, set aside any and all distractions, and then bring your full awareness to your breath is a practice. If you have limiting beliefs about your output and activity as your value, it is a practice that may feel incredibly challenging. Even if that voice in your head has an opinion about sitting doing nothing for ten minutes, do it anyway.

The human mind is one of habit. The more consistently and persistently you practise something new, the easier it becomes to repeat and eventually enjoy. It is useful to pick a similar time every day to do your conscious breathing. It doesn't have to be timed to the last second, but when you are consistent with the time of day, it helps the habit mind to receive the new programming. My personal practice is to get up around 6 a.m., write for two to three hours, and then meditate for 30 minutes. My body knows that somewhere between eight and ten in the morning it will get half an hour to relax and breathe deeply.

If this is a new concept for you, I am not suggesting you dive into meditation straight away. The mind can have all kinds of beliefs about the meaning of *meditation*. Better to get started with something you know you can already do very well - breathe. Equally, if you already have a consistent meditation practice, congratulations, keep it up.

If you would like to feel more deeply relaxed, rested and rejuvenated, I invite you to make the time to sit and breathe consciously for ten minutes every day. What I have come to know about this practice is that, for some people, it may be easier to start with three or five minutes and gradually build up to ten. If your mind is one of those that tells you, "You're too busy to sit and breathe for ten minutes", start with three. Set the egg timer or the clock on your phone, sit in a comfortable chair that you won't fall asleep in, then bring all your attention to your breath within your body. Breathe more deeply, without forcing it, but using the fullness of your diaphragm to fill your body with the breath of life, then slowly release that deep breath and allow your body to feel the release as you allow your shoulders to relax and drop down a little. With each conscious breath feel your body becoming more relaxed, and at the same time notice that you feel a new level of invigoration. You may also start to yawn. The yawning reflex is telling you that your body is getting more oxygen and it's not quite sure what to do with it; it may also indicate that you are not generally getting enough sleep.

Add this breathing practice into your everyday routine. Take time to notice any changes that you feel within your body as you make conscious breathing part of your day. As you grow your consciousness, make other changes in your beliefs, and embody this practice, you will soon be able to recognise differences in your life. There will be a time when you are ready to step into a longer and deeper meditation practice. If you need support with that you may find a local class or group that teaches one of the many forms of meditation. I facilitate groups every week to support people in their meditation practices. I also send out a weekly Monday Mindfulness meditation track to my email list, so be sure you have signed up to receive your weekly practice reminder. You can do that by visiting www.JulietVorster.com.

How much sleep is enough?

How much sleep do you get every night? Do you wake up rested, or more tired than when you went to bed? I remember a time in my life when every morning was miserable. I would be so exhausted that I would fall asleep the minute my head hit the pillow, but within a few short hours I would be wide awake, spending the darkest hours of the night worrying and stressing about events in my life, only to fall asleep again an hour before the alarm went off. Needless to say, at the sound of the alarm, I was not relaxed, rested or ready for a new day. Does that sound familiar? Perhaps you struggle to fall asleep even though you are exhausted. Or maybe you sleep all night, yet awaken feeling tired and grumpy.

Quality sleep is very important to the success of your everyday life. Here are some things that can help you get a better night's sleep:

1. Go to bed earlier. I read somewhere that the sleep you get before midnight is worth twice what you get after midnight. I have tested this theory personally and I can definitely feel the difference when I get off to sleep around 10:30 or 11 p.m. versus those nights that I don't get to sleep until 12:30 or 1 in the morning.

2. Breathe and relax just before going to bed. I know this may seem paradoxical, but taking time to consciously relax your body *before* you go to sleep sets you up for a better night's sleep. Take five minutes before you go to sleep to breathe deeply. Then, starting at your toes and working upwards, invite every part of your body to relax. If you think you may fall asleep doing this exercise, do it in bed, then it doesn't matter if you nod off.

3. The world turns without you. If you are reading the newspaper, listening to the radio news, or watching the TV news just before going to bed, you are stimulating your brain, mostly not in a good way. World events are going to continue without you whilst you sleep, so why would you fill yourself up with worry, anxiety and fear, and take that into dream time with you? It would be better to read or watch something relaxing and soothing just before you go to sleep.

4. Stop scaring yourself. Following on from number three, I have a friend who loves to watch scary movies into the small hours of the night and then wonders why she doesn't sleep well. Your subconscious mind is wide awake whilst your body sleeps. It doesn't know the difference between 'real' and 'tv', so it spends time trying to process and store the information it has just seen. If you really enjoy a good suspense of horror film, watch it and then take half an hour to relax your body and unwind *before* getting into bed.

5. Get more sleep. Opinions vary on how much sleep an adult needs. I find it varies for me depending on what I am eating, and on the level of stress and amount of exercise in my day. On average I need seven hours of quality sleep. You are the expert on you, but you would probably benefit from consistently getting at least six hours of sleep every night. That may mean that you need to manage your schedule differently to ensure you have the time for at least six hours sleep. Try it, you may be astonished how much difference an extra hour of sleep makes to your day.

6. Go back to your youth. When I was a child we had a bedtime routine. It involved the ritual of sitting down with the TV off, having a glass of milk and a biscuit, getting into pyjamas, washing hands and face, brushing hair and teeth, then going to bed and having a chapter of a story read to us. Finally we would be 'tucked in' with our sheets and blankets wrapped tightly around us, kissed goodnight, and lights were put out. What's your bed time routine? If it's rush from one chore to another, do a bit of paper work from the office, hustle the kids into bed, and then finally collapse on the sofa and fall asleep watching TV, perhaps you might want to create a supportive, nurturing and nourishing bedtime routine that gets you nice and relaxed, calm and ready for a full night of peaceful sleep.

7. Self medication does not make for great sleep. I know, it's just a glass or two of wine, how bad can it be? If you are stressed and rushing around, you may be tempted to 'relax' with a glass or two of your favourite tipple before crashing out on the sofa. Alcohol may take the edge off, and in the first instance, may get you off to sleep, but it is a stimulant, and in the long term it will not aid a peaceful night's sleep. Think about changing to a chamomile tea or another relaxing herbal infusion. If the idea of stopping your evening drink makes you feel uncomfortable, you may want to seek some professional support in managing alcohol in your life.

8. Scent makes sense. If you struggle to get off to sleep, you could invest in some lavender, perhaps in the form of a heated cushion or a sachet that you put under your pillow, or even a spray that you put on the bedclothes.

Lavender has been shown to change people's brain waves and induce deeper sleep. Even if you are not overly fond of the smell, it still has the same effect.

You may want to try some or all of these tips, depending on how you're sleeping at the moment. Whichever you decide on, I would definitely encourage you to become more conscious of your bedtime routine and the amount of sleep you are getting. When you are constantly exhausted it is really challenging to ignite success, no matter how you define it.

Not all exercise is created equal

"Training gives us an outlet for suppressed energies created by stress and thus tones the spirit just as exercise conditions the body."

ARNOLD SCHWARZENEGGER

In my youth I relished my time in the gym. I had abs of steel, I was proud of my physical appearance and I set a high value on my body's strength and stamina. Somewhere along the journey of my life my priorities changed and I learned to value my inner strength and stamina more highly. When you read the word exercise, what comes up for you?

We all understand the value of exercising the body. Understanding the need for exercise doesn't mean you have to spend hours sweating in the gym or jogging around city roads. Here is a piece of research that will open your mind to some new beliefs about exercise:

Ellen Langer, a Harvard psychologist, wanted to discover how our perception of the exercise we are getting affects the way our bodies respond. She took 84 hotel maids and quizzed them on how much exercise they took. Almost all said none or very little, which was surprising given how active hotel maids are every hour of their working day. All the maids were in the 'highly active' bracket, but didn't see themselves that way and their bodies reflected the perceived lack of exercise.

Having taken all relevant weights and measurements, Ms Langer divided the maids into two groups. One group was taught that every thing they did was some form of exercise. It was explained to them how many calories each task burned, which muscle groups were being exercised, and how they were living a highly active lifestyle. The other group was given no information.

A month later all the women were weighed and measured again. In the group that had been educated, there was a decrease in their systolic blood pressure, weight, and waist-to-hip ratio, as well as an average ten percent drop in blood pressure across the group.

Unless you are bedridden, the likelihood is you are already getting more exercise than you think. As this study shows, when you change your thinking, you can change your physical health. It is great to start where you are. Think about all the walking, lifting and stretching you already do. If you are not sure how much you walk, get yourself a pedometer and measure the steps you take every day. You will be surprised; I was.

The next step is to think about adding more steps. Reeling from having to find time to sleep more, you may be panicking about now having to find time to exercise. Take a breath, this bit is easier and more fun than you think. Every day you have opportunities to make new choices about your exercise routine without having to go anywhere different or pay for a class. When you become more mindful of nourishing your body in every way it gets easier to remember the new choices.

Here are a few ideas that can add exercise to your day without taking up much time.

- Could you take the stairs instead of the lift (elevator)?

- Could you park three rows further from the door of the supermarket or office?
- Could you walk the children to school instead of taking the car?
- Every time you walk up stairs at home, go up and down an extra time (this can really add some great value exercise to your day).
- Each time you pick something up or lift something a bit heavy, imagine you are lifting weights in the gym, toning your muscles, and melting away fat.

Take these ideas and expand on them. Make it fun to try and think up new ways to recognise you are exercising as you carry out your every day tasks. As always, before you make any changes to your diet and exercise routine, please consult with your general practitioner or physician.

Starting where you are is great and you may be ready to do more. My best advice on what to do next is to only do something that is fun and that you enjoy. Take a dance class, join an aqua-aerobics group, meet up with friends for a speedy walk round the local park. Get creative and do something that works for you. Remember the 3Ps, get into the habit of your new exercise, practise persistently and be patient with your body as you start to see the results.

Chapter 9 Awareness Exercise - Keep a diary

For one month keep a diary of everything you eat and drink, all the relaxation and sleep that you get, and all the different kinds of exercise you take. Simply thinking about these things will not give you an accurate picture. When we record information we learn so much more. Remember this is about awareness, not an opportunity for judgement and criticism. I expect that you'll be really surprised by your findings.

To make your life easier, I have created some templates for this exercise. Go to 'www.JulietVorster.com/ISBB-downloads' to download your sheets.

Once you have collected all this information, you can decide in which areas you'd like to do something different, and what that *different* might look like. You may even notice during the month that your habits have changed simply because you have become more mindful of the choices you are making.

Nourishing Your Suitcase

Chapter 10

LIVING ON THE BAGGAGE CONVEYOR

"People are like dirt. They can either
nourish you and help you grow as a
person or they can stunt your growth
and make you wilt and die."

~ PLATO

There have been many times in my life when I thought my life would be far better if I were living on an island. Preferably one surrounded with barbed wire, a very long way from anyone else. Thankfully those days are long gone, and whilst I still enjoy time alone, I am delighted by the richness of relationships that I share with people all around the world. Have you ever felt that living alone, a very long way from any other people, would solve all your problems?

As much as some of us would like to be an island, humans are actually social animals. Just like dogs and horses, our natural inclination is to be part of a tribe. We operate best when we build collaboration and community. There is a longing in us all for great friends, supportive family and intimate lovers. Yet somehow many people experience a world populated by lonely, unsupported, disconnected people. What do you think all your relationships have in common? Is it that you have common beliefs, or attend the same workplace? Do you enjoy the same hobbies, or drink in the same pub? Is there a musical connection, or did you all have your children at the same time? Whilst some or all of these may be true, the one common thing in every relationship is **you**.

It is unfortunate that many of us have early life experiences which create unsupportive beliefs about other people and relationship building. After my first heartbreak as a teenager my mantra was "up drawbridge, down portcullis", which refers to the entrance of a castle. No-one could get past the barriers I put up to protect myself. Of course, there is a fundamental flaw in this thinking - eventually what we put around us as protection ends up imprisoning us. Had I moved to my island with the barbed wire, I wonder how soon I'd have recognised that I was the prisoner?

The common thread in all our relationships is us. When we start to change from the inside out, all our relationships change. This is more good news. You don't have to run around cleaning up every relationship you have. All you have to do is sit still and uncover more layers of yourself. We have already spoken about the mental and emotional atmosphere, or energy field, we have around us constantly. As we ignite greater success by changing our thinking and embracing beliefs that are more supportive, that atmosphere changes and we project different energy. The people around us subtly sense those changes even if they don't immediately notice any substantial changes. As others experience us differently, they react differently, and thus the entire nature of the relationship changes.

This became most apparent to me after I attended my first residential intensive self discovery week. The work we did that week enabled me to release lots of long-held, stuck emotion and move into forgiveness, both for myself and many others in my life. When I came home I really was a different person. My heart had opened in a new way and I was forever changed. Although I knew something had shifted, I didn't really comprehend the depth of the changes until much later. What I did notice was the difference in the way other people treated me. Expressions of affection, such as hugs, which had never been offered before, abounded. People seemed to be far more engaged with me and generally more open. Of course, what I now know is they hadn't changed, I had. I was finally open to receive their affection and embrace the connections that were offered.

As Plato wisely reminds us in the opening quote, people are all kinds of things. We each have within us the power to uplift and nourish as well as the power to crush and wither the people we meet. When we awaken to our own power it gets easier to remember that we choose how we show up and how we behave. Gradually we come to recognise that the beliefs we have adopted are not fundamental truths, but rather opinions synthesised through mistaken interpretations of experiences. With willingness, intention and knowledge, those old beliefs can be weeded out, and fresh seeds of supportive beliefs can be planted.

Take a moment to think about all the people you have some form of relationship with. I'm not only referring to the intimate kinds of relationships, but every kind. Who did you think of first? Typically we think of those closest to us: our partner, parents, children, siblings, best friends. Then we move out to our daily life: colleagues, bosses, neighbours, suppliers, clients, teachers, acquaintances, and so this list goes on, moving outward from the intimate relationships to the casual. As we think about the nature of our different relationships we could almost plot an expanding spiral out from the centre, but what is the centre? What is it that acts as the hub for this spiral of connections? When I answer that question I see the similarity to an artichoke - at the centre of all your relationships you find your heart. The less connected you feel to a person, the less love you feel for them. You and your heart are the hub for all your relationships.

We may not feel the same level of connection or love for

everyone. But we do have some form of relationship with all the people we meet. From the supermarket checkout person to the bank clerk, from the receptionist at the vets to the petrol pump attendant, we have some form of relationship. Every interaction creates a connection which may be the beginning of a life long friendship, or may only be a passing word. What kind of person are you in your relationships? Does who you are, and how you act, change depending on whom you are with? Oh, and did you include the most important relationship on your list? Did you include the one with yourself? Ultimately, it is our relationship with the Self that is the only one we need to work on. When we have a full and complete relationship with ourselves, every other relationship falls into place beautifully.

When we think of the 'Self', who is it we think of? Who is currently reading this book? "I am." Okay but who are you? Perhaps a better question to ask would be "Who do you think you are?" or perhaps, "Who do you believe yourself to be?". I find it strange when I step back inside my mind and realise that the 'Me' that is within my body, the one who observes the world through my eyes, is changeless. I don't feel any different inside myself now than I did when I was 10 or 25 or 40. That which I identify as 'Me' hasn't changed. The conscious, aware, focussing me is always the same. I learn new things, I experience more life, but that part of me which is the observer of my life, beyond the emotions and drama, that part is changeless. Yet all the while the physical elements of me are changing second by second. So much so that every seven years I am completely renewed. Every cell in my body has died and replaced itself. My body is just carbon, and it's a perfectly designed vehicle to allow 'Me' to experience this great adventure called life.

I mentioned in the previous chapter my idea that the body is like a suitcase. A simple carrying device for our true, highest and changeless self. I now invite you to dive into this idea a little deeper with me. Imagine yourself in the baggage claim hall of a major airport. You are standing in front of the carousel as it trundles around. Eventually the various bags and cases start to tumble down the chute and you watch eagerly for your bags to arrive. As you seek your own luggage you also idly notice the wide variety of cases that rattle past you. Some are the most expensive brands, Louis Vuitton or Chanel, all new and pristine. Others are the 'thousand milers' that have been around the world, all battered, with tape holding them together and interesting stickers covering every side. Then there is a vast array of every kind of suitcase, rolling bag, ruck-sack, box and carrying case you could possibly imagine. They come in interesting colours, with bright patterns and they come in black with ribbons and tags and markers so that the owners might pick them out from the sea of other black bags. And despite all these fascinating, obvious demonstrations of diversity, there is still a mystery rattling around on the luggage carousel. What's inside the bags?

If you saw a Louis Vuitton and what I call a 'thousand miler', what story would you make up about the varying contents in the different bags? Would you imagine them both to contain all the same things, or would you imagine that the fancy Louis Vuitton might contain all kinds of lavish and expensive items? Equally, would you look at the 'thousand miler', all battered and stuck together, and imagine the contents might be something more in alignment with the look of the outside? The story you make up about the contents of these two imaginary cases will be influenced by what you believe. You may have been a world traveller and had a bag similar to either of our examples, in which case you might believe it has similar contents to your bag. Your beliefs about money could influence your story about either of the cases. If you have one view about money, you may judge the 'thousand miler' as a terrible thing. If you have a different view about money, you may judge the Louis Vuitton to be a total waste of money. Remember there is no right or wrong, simply your beliefs created from your life experience. There is only one way to know what the contents of the case may be. You have to open it.

When you think about people and their *body suitcases*, how often do you make up stories about the contents based on what the case looks like? In life we are not only the observer of the baggage carousel, we are on it. Jostling and shuffling, shoulder to shoulder with all the other bags and cases. Ideally we want peace and harmony with the others in our life. We all want to have great relationships.

Judgement and comparison are huge barriers to creating great relationships, yet we all get caught up in them in many different ways. When we are judging another, we are indirectly judging ourselves.

Next we tumble into the abyss of comparison, where we almost always come up short as we measure ourselves against the other. There are a couple of things that need some deeper thought here:

1. **There is a difference between** *criticism and judgement* **versus** *discernment and awareness.*

   a. *Criticism* or *judgement* indicates that there is something bad or wrong with the person or situation. You have an opinion (judgement) which makes the other person *less than* in some way. However *discernment* or *awareness* is a measured or intuitive assessment of a person or situation that informs you how to proceed without it being good, bad, right or wrong.

   b. For example: Your best friend hooks you up on a blind date. You meet your date, who is drop-dead gorgeous and super fit. They are dressed immaculately in the latest style. You may *judge* that they are shallow and self-obsessed just from looking at them. This makes them wrong and in some way *less than,* purely based on your snap shot opinion.

c. You decide *not* to run a mile from this 'shallow egotist' and as the evening unfolds and you get chatting, you realise your date is actually intelligent, articulate and engaging. However by the end of the night you recognise (or discern) that the conversation became more limited, you didn't share very much in common, and as lovely as your date is, they are not *The One.* This discernment doesn't make your date good, bad, right or wrong, it is the simple recognition that they are not for you.

d. Evaluating a person or situation without falling into judgement and criticism is part of a healthy decision-making process. We do occasionally meet people who do not necessarily have honourable intentions and there are situations which we don't want to involve ourselves with. That is where discernment is useful. Using judgement in those situations only separates and divides.

2. **When you compare yourself to another it's like comparing a banana with a lemon.**

a. To compare yourself with anyone else is not meaningful because you are each individuals. Just like the lemon and the banana, there is something similar in appearance - in the fruit example they are both mostly yellow, and in your comparison you are both human. That is where the common ground ends. If you were to use a lemon in a recipe calling for a banana you would be very surprised and probably disappointed by the results.

b. When you compare yourself to anyone else, you are comparing what you believe about yourself, based on all your fears, insecurities and shortcomings, with what you believe about the other based on what you see on the outside. Just like the example of the suitcase contents, you have no idea what is going on inside another person. Thus there is absolutely no value in comparing yourself with anyone else. You are your own unique and perfect expression of Life. You are beyond comparison.

Letting go of judgement is definitely an opportunity for growth and learning that takes practise. The habit mind has become so well conditioned to judge others that the thoughts are formed and the words are in our minds before we can blink. It is possible to get better at stopping the first reaction of judgement, but for now, let's start where we are and recognise that once the opinion is formed in the mind as a thought, you still have a choice. You can wallow in the muddy pond of judgement and continue focussing on those critical thoughts. Alternatively, you can gently allow conscious awareness of the judgmental and critical thoughts and then you can do these two things:

First you can very deliberately choose to change the thought. For example, you may see someone walking down the street dressed very differently to the way you are and your chatter voice immediately comes up with something like this, "Look at the state of that. What on earth are they wearing? They look a right mess dressed like that." With intentional thought you could change that to something more like this, "Oh, that's a very different way of dressing to mine, how interesting it is that there is so much diversity in the world."

The second thing to do is some personal enquiry. Using this example, you might ask yourself something like, "What is it about someone dressing in that way, which is very different to my way, that makes me so uncomfortable?" As you contemplate this question you may discover all kinds of unexpected answers. Perhaps you realise that this kind of reaction is simply an unconscious repetition of something your mother always said. Perhaps you discover that you feel very restricted about being your authentic, creative self. Seeing someone else expressing themselves through their clothing, doing something you don't believe you can, may press your insecurity buttons and cause this critical reaction. Just like all the beliefs we have about everything, there are myriad things to know about why we think and behave the way we do. Always remembering that this form of self enquiry, just like the exercises at the end of each chapter, is all about self awareness. This is *not* your chance to turn judgement and criticism in on yourself.

Building great relationships is all about creating genuine connection. Opening an energetic space where people can feel safe, accepted and welcome. Much of our learned behaviour focusses on separation from others rather than connection to them. We are taught to compete from a very early age, but few of us were taught how to collaborate until much later in our education.

When we constantly judge and criticise, it is difficult to build strong, authentic relationships in any area of life. This applies to ourselves and to others. We will always be operating from an internal setting of *not enough* if our belief system (who we think we are, how worthy or valuable we think we are, and how the world will treat us) is based on criticism and judgement. This becomes the energy information we are broadcasting and so we get back what we put out, even though we may be totally unaware of it. Through our energy we draw into our experience repeating patterns of behaviour from those around us. How many times have you had a new boss who has treated you the same way as the previous one? It's a different person, but with the same attitude. What about a new lover who turned out to be just like the last one, who turned out to be just like your Mum or Dad? With all the advantage of hindsight, I can see very clearly that my first two partners had similarities to my Dad. We keep on experiencing similar people and situations because we are unknowingly sending out our beliefs, and the intelligence of the Universe returns to us exactly what we put out. Our new project is to work on ourselves with greater compassion so we can transform our hidden beliefs. Simultaneously we can learn to use our powerful mind more consciously, so we are intentionally creating our life, not simply bobbing around like a piece of flotsam adrift on the ocean.

"What you think of me is none of my business."

~ TERRY COLE WHITTAKER

Strong external relationships depend on a strong internal relationship

I used to think of myself as a chameleon. My personality would change depending on who I was with. Have you ever done that? Do you ever wonder why?

In my case, again with the gift of hindsight, I can recognise that I was afraid that who I was didn't measure up and that I would be 'found out'. In corporate circles there is something known as 'impostor syndrome'. This is a belief system in which senior executives, people at the top of the ladder, believe that they aren't really good enough to hold the position, believing they lack the requisite skills and ability, and sooner or later they will be discovered as a fraud or 'impostor'. This belief system can gradually erode all self-confidence and lead to a mental breakdown or a genuine failure at work, thus becoming a self-fulfilling prophecy. Our thoughts and beliefs are that powerful.

Embracing the above quote from Terry Cole Whittaker, which is actually a title from one of her books, is something to practise. It is not about a false arrogance. It speaks to a genuine realisation that the only person you can possibly be is you. Everyone you meet is going to have an opinion about you, and, sorry to break the bad news, you can't do a thing about it. Expending time and energy in an effort to please or placate others is exhausting. Most often you end up satisfying no-one and feeling rotten yourself. Equally, trying to second guess what others think about you and trying to adapt yourself to meet your perceived belief about their expectation is a road to disaster. Have you ever watched a scene in a movie when the eager young man meets his girlfriend's father for the first time and is desperately trying to impress? It makes us squirm in our seats with embarrassment for him. We feel the insecurity and fear of the young man. Because we are all constantly receiving the energy signals broadcast from others, we feel, or sense, when someone is being inauthentic. Working on our personal relationship with ourselves first is the best way to build spectacular relationships with everyone else. When we become content with who we are, even though we still have areas within ourselves we want to work on, we show up with authenticity, humility and compassion. This is an irresistible package. Think about who you would rather spend time with, people who are calm, centred and know who they are? Or people who are neurotic, fearful and trying desperately to fit in?

As humans, once our basic needs are met, we all really want the same things. We want to be loved and valued. We want to feel fulfilled and we want to make a difference. Recognising this, and remembering it, allows us to move beyond the physical differences and build stronger connections with each other. In my experience, we also have the same insecurities. We fear we are not enough on some level, and this belief leads us to fear rejection from the tribe. The ancient part of our psyche, often called the *reptilian brain*, recognises that being outside the tribe almost certainly means death. As an individual it was virtually impossible to defend yourself from the local sabre-tooth tiger, but as a tribe, there was a chance you might all survive. Even though this particular scenario is no longer a possibility, being part of a community is a deep human need. Babies who don't receive human contact will frequently fail to thrive and in some cases die without having a specific diagnosis or disease. We are hard-wired for connections, and this programming causes us to adapt who and how we are so that we will be accepted into the tribe of our birth or the tribe of our choice.

Just for a moment, put your hand over your heart and take in a deep breath. Who do you think you are? Do you define yourself by the roles, successes and things that you have? Or do you have a confident sense of who you are, anchored in self-acceptance and compassion, free from judgement and criticism? Are you able to go even deeper and become aware of your inner observer, the changeless, timeless part of you that feels just the same now as you did at seven or ten years old? Having compassion for the physical elements of who you are whilst also going deeper into the Self is a road to success on every level.

No matter what your answers are, it is possible for you to build a stronger sense of self, to become more self-accepting and self-compassionate, if you choose.

Let's start right now. Say out loud:

"I am an okay person. I love and allow myself to be loved. I give and receive in perfect balance. I accept myself just as I am right now. I easily choose thoughts that nourish and support me. I am willing to change."

This is a great starting point. If you recognise that you would love to be more confident and comfortable in your own skin, repeat this affirmation frequently. Allow the words to wash over you and trust that the process of metamorphosis is underway.

The world is a perfect mirror, you always get back what you give out.

"Life is a mirror and it will reflect back to the thinker what he (she) thinks into it."

~ ERNEST HOLMES

We are all looking for acceptance, approval and love, consciously or subconsciously. But how can we expect to find it from others when we don't give it to ourselves? To discover the areas where you are least loving, accepting and approving of yourself, all you need to do is look around you at the people in your life. Each one of them is reflecting back to you what you are giving out in some way. Do you notice all the critical people, the angry people, or do you notice the happy people? What irritates you most in others? Everything you discover brings you something greater to know about yourself and your beliefs. There is a flip side to this practice. What do you most admire in people that you know? You wouldn't be able to see those good things, if you didn't already have them within yourself. So be gentle. Make sure you don't fall further into the hole of judgement. Take time to celebrate all the good that you are already aware of within your fabulous self.

Seeking The One

When it comes to relationships, many people I work with are looking for 'The One', and I don't mean God. They seek the perfect partner, soul mate, lover with whom they imagine spending the rest of their lives. If this is something you are seeking, I have one question for you: Who do you need to become to be the perfect partner for the one you are seeking? This isn't about 'acting' in a certain way, but rather about becoming the genuine and authentic person you need to be in order to attract the partner of your dreams. Frequently we become so externally focussed in our search for the perfect mate we forget that even if we find one, they also have to be attracted to us. Use the idea of the universal mirror to notice what you see being reflected back to you concerning your beliefs about relationships and the 'perfect' partner. You may discover that even though you want a strong, empathic, communicative, gorgeous, loving partner, you have some beliefs about how possible that is (or not) for you.

In leading many groups I have discovered that some of us believe good things can happen to other people, but they are less likely to happen to us. Check in with yourself on anything you would love in your life. How possible do you actually believe it is? Do you believe you really can be in the most wonderful relationship with the partner of your dreams? Or would you start to worry about how soon things might go wrong, doubt that they really feel the way they say they do, or wonder what they are doing when they work late? Would you fall into the belief of 'this is too good to be true'? It is possible for this belief to raise its head in any situation, particularly as we change our beliefs and start to see improvements in everyday life. I have had many similar conversations with clients over the years. When I ask them how things are working for them, they tell me things are good, but they have a worried expression on their faces which doesn't match the words. As I quiz them about their apparent concerns, the answer is always a variation of the same thing. "I'm having a great time, things are going really well, but I'm worried that they will change because nothing good lasts forever."

Nothing good lasts forever, is that one of your beliefs? When we believe that every bit of *good* has to be balanced out with some *bad* then it's no wonder the divorce rate is so high. Scale up that theory and it's possible to see why countries go to war. It's a belief, and if you choose to subscribe to it, then it will definitely be true for you. If you recognise this belief as something active in your mind, and you'd like to change it, use something like this as a reprogramming tool:

"I can experience as much good as I choose. I now choose to allow the good in my life to grow and expand. I seek only good, trusting that I am always in the perfect flow of life."

Remember, you are the only thinker in your mind. You get to decide if you are going to remain clinging to what you have always known or if you are going to let go of the old and open up to igniting success beyond your old beliefs.

As we have already discovered, our minds are complex things and the rewiring process is just like tending a garden, we need constant vigilance for the weeds. Pulling up the weeds of old beliefs is an ongoing practice. Those weeds keep you stuck and hold you back from the success you seek. Each time we pluck them from our minds, we go a little deeper, liberating something more from our belief system, which sets us free to soar higher.

Every relationship is The One

I recently saw this quote from Byron Katie, "My experience is that I don't need anyone to complete me. As soon as I realize that, everyone completes me." Often, as we seek our perfect partner, we fall into thinking they will somehow complete us and make us whole. Does that mean you are only half a person, or two thirds of a person, when you are single? No. Coming full circle in this chapter, the only relationship you really need to improve is the one with that gorgeous creature you see in the mirror every morning. When you are comfortable with who you are and where you are in life, when you recognise and embody your fundamental, innate wholeness, then every person you connect with becomes one with you.

Chapter 10 Awareness Exercise - Claiming Your Magnificence

As we recognise the pivotal role each of us plays in all our relationships, let's take a moment to break through our inner guilt, blame and shame. It's time to claim your magnificence.

1. List ten things you like about yourself.
2. List ten things you are good at.
3. List ten ways you are a good friend.
4. List ten ways you make a difference in the world.
5. Ask 10 people you love and trust to complete these lists about you.

You may have been doing okay with this exercise until you read number five. Breathe. There will be a temptation to skip that last request. I encourage you, most lovingly, to be brave and ask people to complete these lists about you. You will be amazed at the answers you get.

If you take the challenge you will have 440 positive statements about yourself. I want you to do one more thing. I want you to read all of them and then synthesise them down into a manifesto for your life.

Today I _____(your name here)_____, claim my magnificence.

I now recognise that I am ____ (put at least 10 of the statements from your lists)

_____

_____

_____

I know that I am the perfect me. I am always evolving and growing. I practise weeding my thought garden and I easily release the beliefs that no longer serve me. I am willing to love and accept myself exactly as I am. I allow myself space to grow as I give up any old stories that limit my success.

I take time each day to practise the things that lift me up and nourish me. I remember that 'No.' is a complete sentence. I claim my own power and remember that I am beyond comparison, I am magnificent.

"I am an okay person. I love and allow myself to be loved. I give and receive in perfect balance. I accept myself just as I am right now. I easily choose thoughts that nourish and support me. I am willing to change."

Signed _____ Date _____

You can find copies of this declaration, in pdf, Word and Pages on my website: www.JulietVorster.com/ISBB-downloads.

Living On The Baggage Conveyor

Chapter 11

BELIEF BUSTING IN YOUR VOCATIONAL LIFE

*"Opportunity is missed by most
people because it is dressed in
overalls and looks like work."*

~ THOMAS A. EDISON

The alarm goes off, another day dawns, and the first conscious thought in your mind is, "Oh no, it's Monday and I *have* to go to work." The feeling of dread fills your body and you start wondering if you could get away with asking your partner to call in sick on your behalf, like your Mum used to do on a test day at school. Does this sound like your life? When it comes to work, or your beliefs about work, are you surviving or thriving?

I'm grateful to have had very few of these days in my life. On the odd occasion I started to feel like this about a job I was usually in a position to quickly leave and do something that fills my heart. But I do know what they feel like. There are few things in life that erode one's joy quite as fast as feeling trapped in the need to earn money, and the belief that you have to *work hard* to do it.

You may experience these same feelings of dread even if you are not getting up and *going to work.* Perhaps you are a stay-at-home parent who really isn't enjoying the role, in which case not only do you feel the challenge of your 'job', you also feel guilty because you 'should' want to be with your children. And then again, you may desperately want a job, but be struggling to find one. You wake up with a sense of despondency which may also be topped up with fear about money and how you will pay your way.

When it comes to work, career, vocation, jobs and service, we humans have a whole bunch of beliefs that keep us limited, playing small and being miserable. "Yes, but..." I hear you shout, "I have to work, or I cannot live!" Really, is that true? And even if it is true, does that mean you have to do something that makes you miserable eight to ten hours a day for the rest of your life? Or perhaps what we need to do first is redefine 'work'.

The Oxford Dictionary says that work is an *activity involving mental or physical effort done in order to achieve a result*. It also says that work is *a task or tasks to be undertaken*. Nowhere in that definition does it say anything about dread, misery, fulfillment, satisfaction or joy. So when you think about *work* what thoughts and beliefs come up? What did you see modelled by your family? There are families in some areas of the UK where no-one, across three generations, has ever had a job. The previous industries in the area have all collapsed and there are no jobs.

You may be reading that and wishing it was you, but think for a moment about the sense of purpose and motivation you get from *having* to go to work every day. Think of the opportunity to socialise, expand your knowledge, make new connections and feel valued. I can't imagine how different life would be if I had never had the vast array of experiences I've had in my working career. Even when I worked in what I call a *day job* (working for someone else), there was always something to engage my attention and bring me a moment of joy. Could you be grateful for your job? Whether you love it or loathe it, could you take a moment to see some good in it and be grateful? This invitation applies if you have a traditional job or if you volunteer, are a stay-at-home parent, or if your current situation doesn't include a job. Can you be grateful for the things you do in everyday life?

I invite you to move into gratitude because when we appreciate something, we are creating a positive energy about it. We are training our mind to look for more good. And when we think about an asset 'appreciating,' we imagine it growing; so what we appreciate appreciates, it grows. Developing an attitude of gratitude also puts you in a more positive frame of mind and helps you seek the good in situations.

Let the good feeling guide you

"Follow your bliss."

~ JOSEPH CAMPBELL

I'm a big fan of doing what I love. At almost every stage of my corporate career I have enjoyed a sense of fulfillment. Even in stressful jobs, I have been doing work that I have enjoyed. If that's not currently true for you, what does your ideal work look and feel like? Try not to think about the tiny detail, but rather look at the bigger picture. In your ideal work:

- How would you love to feel when you arrive at work each day?
- What difference could you imagine making with your work?
- What would the people that you work with be like?
- How many hours, during what time of day, would you love to work?
- What kind of space would you love to work in?
- How would you like to feel about yourself when you get your pay cheque?

You may have a preference such as working with children, creating things with your hands or leading others. That's great.

Ideally you don't want to zoom your focus in to the daily detail of the exact work, the location, the specifics of hours and money. Putting too much detail around these things can restrict your possibilities. I have found that Life has a much better imagination than I do. My small human imagination could not have dreamed up many of the magnificent experiences I have had.

I was once invited to work on a six week contract to help out an old employer of mine. I was grateful for the job and I very much enjoyed it. Within a very short space of time I was taken on full time as the assistant manager, and within eighteen months I was running the contract. I could never have foreseen that possibility, and, at the time, I could not have believed I was capable of taking on that kind of senior role. Life, in its infinite intelligence, had a better imagination than I. When it comes to your creation, don't limit yourself by imagineering something you think you can get. It's time to go beyond your beliefs and allow greater good into your life.

Why do you do what you do all day?

This might seem like a silly question, but have you ever asked yourself? The first answer that comes up is usually some variation of, "Because I have to." But that's not really true, no-one makes you do what you do. Even though it may not feel like much of an option, on some level you choose what you do all day. I once heard a speaker explaining this idea that everything is a choice. He told us that we could decide to sit in the chair we are in and not get up, ever. If we made that choice, firstly things would probably get damp and smelly, and eventually people in white coats would come and remove us, take us to a secure unit, clean us up, feed us and put us in a padded cell. It's a choice and, as with every choice, there is a result. The classic idea of cause and effect. You choose what you do with your day (the cause), and as a result you experience all that you experience (the effect).

Allow your mind and heart to open as you contemplate some more answers to this question. Why do you do what you do all day? What is it that you want to experience as a result of what you do all day? You may not be getting those things yet, but this is the time to evaluate where you are, letting go of any judgement or criticism. Then decide where you want to be. Pause for a moment and jot down a few answers to these questions. Allow your mind to open to some new possibilities.

In the first twenty years of my working life I bounced from one thing to the next like a pinball because I could do the work. I enjoyed what I did, I was good at what I did, but it was never a conscious choice. As I awakened to new possibilities in my life, I started evaluating where I was, and where I wanted to be. Not just with regard to work and career, but in every area of my life. When I started to learn about human potential and how to enable others to grow and expand, that was when I discovered my true passion and purpose. From then on, I really started following my bliss. Now I trust my inner guidance, based on what lights me up from the inside, what inspires me to move forward into new projects and fabulous adventures. This is your opportunity to do just that for yourself. It doesn't mean you have to throw everything in the air and walk away from your life. It is an opportunity to become conscious and mindful of the beliefs you hold and the choice you make because of those beliefs. As you gain awareness, you have the tools to change your beliefs and make new choices.

If that voice in your head is chatting away telling you it's not possible for you to change in this way, just take a moment to have a dialogue with it. Thank it for sharing and let it know that you are safe, and that you are working with something different for now. If consciously engaging in an inner dialogue is something new for you it may seem a little strange at first, but stick with it. As you become more mindful and aware of your thoughts and the inner chatter, it gets easier and easier to have a conversation with yourself that allows the highest part of you to be the director of operations. The part of our mind we are dialoguing with is often called the ego. Some teachers say the ego is a terrible thing. Personally I think the ego has a role to play in our lives. It's the thing that gets us out of bed in the morning. It's the motivation to achieve and the part of our mind that helps keep us safe by recognising potential threats. The difficulty with the ego, if we allow it to run the show, is that it can have an over-developed expectation of fear and threat, which can sometimes keep us stuck in false beliefs. Simultaneously, it creates balance and motivation when being properly directed by the highest part of your mind. If we had all moved beyond the ego there would be no point in being here. We'd all be sitting around in saffron, white or gold robes, meditating on the Self and doing nothing else.

Whilst I believe the ego has a place in your life, that place is not as the captain of the ship. It is better suited to the role of deck hand. A part of your mind that does what you ask, rather than trying to run the show. One of the jobs of the ego is to keep you alive in your body. The ego has a very limited world view and believes that you are born and you die. That may also be your belief, which is perfect for you. I believe that we are never born and we never die. I believe that our soul, spirit, life force, consciousness, or whichever word works for you, is eternal and infinite. We come into these disposable human suitcases for a grand adventure and when we're done, the carbon unit of our body stops working and we return to the Infinite, back to where we came from. I'm not here to sell you any particular belief system, but rather to invite you, again and again, to evaluate and better understand your beliefs, where they came from, and more importantly, how they are influencing your life now. From that place of greater awareness, you are able to make different choices and ignite new levels of success in every area of your life.

I work because I need the money

"Money is only a tool. It will take you wherever you wish, but it will not replace you as the driver."

~ AYN RAND

We will dive deep into money beliefs in the next chapter, but the idea that "I work because I need the money" is probably the most common answer to the question 'why do you do what you do all day?'

Is money the only reason you work? If I were to pay you the same amount of money as you currently receive, would you do something different? Would you spend all day cleaning public toilets? As you read this, your answer may be, "I do that all day already." However, your answer is more likely to be "no". Especially when it comes to cleaning public toilets all day. Which tells us that it's not all about the money. Although we most often default into thinking we work for money, research suggests that we do what we do for many other reasons. Some of those reasons are good and valid, some are based on old, limiting beliefs that may no longer serve the new vision for our life.

What answers came to mind when you started thinking about your ideal work and answering the questions earlier in this chapter?

- Did you imagine feeling fulfilled by the work and service you give?

- Did you think about feeling valued by colleagues and leaders for the work you do?

- Were you able to envision working with people who supported you, were collaborative and creative and who loved their work just as much as you do?

- Could you imagine working hours that fitted your lifestyle perfectly, without having to manipulate the system?

- Did you allow your mind to expand into the possibility of spending all your time in a healthy working environment with an abundance of natural light, good sound ambience, and plenty of space to relax and breathe?

As you review your answers for these questions, you will come to recognise that you want much more than money in exchange for the things you do with your day (or night). Having worked for over twenty years in the printing and document management arena, many of the locations in which I worked were dark and dingy. Print rooms are frequently established in the basement of buildings with no natural light and poor sound management. I was delighted when I moved into management and had my first corner office. Prior to that experience it was quite difficult for me to imagine a better working environment because I had no reference point for what that might look and feel like.

Perhaps, as we have been talking about creating a better life, you have been struggling to imagine what that could look and feel like. Without a reference point, it can sometimes be quite difficult to imagine, particularly if you are more of a logical, practical thinker. One of the best ways I have found to help myself overcome the limits of my imagination and the limited expectations I have acquired in my life, is to create a vision board. Sometimes called a 'dream board', the idea is to tap into other people's imaginations by finding pictures that symbolise or represent what you would love to be, do or have in your own life. There is a full description and a short guided visualisation to lead you through the process of creating your own vision board at the end of the chapter.

"Vision is the art of seeing what is invisible to others."

~ JONATHAN SWIFT

What would you want if you didn't have to be disappointed about not getting it?

One of the observations I hear frequently when I teach or coach is that people don't want to dream big for fear of being disappointed when things don't materialise. Which makes this question all the more powerful. When you think about doing work and service that you love and are excited to do, can you dream your dream *and* let go of being disappointed if you don't get exactly what you want? Can you let go of *needing* to have whatever you want and instead bathe in the joy of dreaming, all the while staying happy in the now? For some, this is a big ask. Life may have been one big series of disappointments and the thought of exposing yourself to another one may seem a leap too far.

When I don't get something I want, I sometimes make up a story about the meaning of not receiving it. When you don't get something you desire, what story do you make up about yourself? Could it be that you remember being told that you *don't deserve* to have this or that when you were a young child? Or did you experience a disappointment so monumentally heartbreaking that you made a subtle vow to never expose yourself to that kind of pain again? The human mind is very complex. There are many possible reasons why you may believe or feel the way you do about being disappointed. Are you willing to change? If this feels relevant to you, you may not know exactly how to overcome this fear. The important question is, are you willing to change your belief system and open to a greater possibility for your life? In fact that is the most important question for all of us to ask ourselves if we are looking for something greater in our life. "Am I willing to change?" We can't avoid change, in every moment cells are dying in our body and new ones are bursting into life. The world turns, the seasons change, the universal imperative remains: Grow or die. Change is the very essence of new creation and growth.

We have already looked at the power of the words we use. Disappointment often comes at the other end of an expectation. When we start to dream about a new job, or perfect partner, we often set expectations around our vision. We think it must be this or that. Whilst there is some benefit to being specific with what we want, getting mentally and emotionally attached to a certain, very specific, outcome takes away from the rich imagination of infinite potential. This is the reason for using mostly feeling-based questions rather than result-based questions when I asked you about your ideal job. The Universe is a realm of vast unlimited energy. When we start to get specific about the look and everyday detail of what we want and how it should reveal itself in our lives, we are taking the infinite down an ever-narrowing chute into a few very limited options.

Imagine you are listening to a magic radio, on which you have digital radio, medium wave, long wave and FM frequencies. You can switch between all of them and listen to myriad stations playing all kinds of music and talk shows. When you decide on a specific type of music, you can tell the radio what you want to listen to, but when you do, everything other than what you've chosen vanishes from the radio. (Did I mention it was a magic radio?)

As an example, you decide that you only want to listen to country music. You tell the radio about your decision and all the other options disappear from your radio. Then you decide that you only want to listen to New Country. Once again all the other stations vanish. Then you decide that you only want to listen to the very latest New Country music, songs that have been released in the last 12 months. The remaining stations that play older Country vanish.

A few weeks later you realise that you want greater diversity in your musical entertainment but now everything else has vanished from your radio and you are stuck with the very latest New Country music. You feel disappointed that you can't have greater variety and observe that what remains no longer feeds your soul.

Alternatively, you could have had a different conversation with your magic radio. If at the beginning you had said to your radio something like, "I want to listen to music that makes me feel relaxed and happy. I want to be able to hear and understand the lyrics and I don't want it to be too loud." With this request your magic radio could bring you everything from Motown through Mozart with some Tim McGraw thrown in for good measure. You would always have diversity and be entertained in a way that matches your true desires.

This is exactly what happens when we get too attached to specific expectations around our desires. We limit the Infinite and then become disappointed with what we get. Or wonder why it takes so long to receive what we've asked for and feel disappointed because it's not here yet. You will read some other views on the subject of being specific. I can only tell you about my experience and the results of my personal experimentation. My best advice is for you to conduct your own experiments and discover what brings you the most satisfactory results.

Busting the myth of hard work and success

> *"Work is love made visible. And if you cannot work*
> *with love but only with distaste, it is better that you*
> *should leave your work and sit at the gate of the temple*
> *and take alms of those who work with joy."*
>
> ~ KHALIL GIBRAN

I'm sure you have, at some time in your life, heard or been told that you have to work hard to be successful. This, too, is a belief. It's up to you if you wish to believe it or not. There are many books already written about this myth. My favourite is *The 4-Hour Work Week* by Timothy Ferris. In the introduction to his engaging book, he says this:

"People don't want to be millionaires — they want to

experience what they believe only millions can buy. Ski chalets, butlers, and exotic travel often enter the picture. Perhaps rubbing cocoa butter on your belly in a hammock while you listen to waves rhythmically lapping against the deck of your thatched-roof bungalow?"

What do you think? Sounds good to me. Tim Ferris works less than four hours per week and manages to do all these things. And he is not the only one. He is part of a new culture that has moved beyond the old paradigm of work and save, work and save, working until you can eventually retire and hoping you will live long enough to enjoy your savings. Hard work is a belief, a myth we have been educated into. Always remembering that the people around us cannot teach us something they do not know, we have the opportunity to let go of our old beliefs and move into a new paradigm of possibilities.

You might want to take a deep breath right now. This is one of the big beliefs many of us have. Breaking through it is a process. I invite you to take some time to think about all the beliefs you have about 'working for a living'. One of mine used to be 'I can't make great money doing what I love'. Fortunately I have been able to release that and live the life of my dreams doing work and service that fills me up in every way.

Keep in mind that all these things are only beliefs, you weren't born with them, you have learned them. And, if you choose, you can un-learn them and set yourself free.

Chapter 11 - Awareness Exercise: Create your own vision board

I love leading this exercise with a group, it's so much fun. The energy of people gathered with a common aim - to grow themselves and their lives - enables everyone to catch the breeze of the collective enthusiasm. Whenever we come together in groups to do this kind of work, it enlivens the whole experience and takes the energy to a greater level. You may want to get some friends or your family together to take part in this exercise.

To create a vision board you need several things:

1. A large piece of cardboard. You decide how big you want your board to be. You could use the side of a grocery box or some larger packaging. You don't have to go to the art store and buy an expensive piece of board, but you can if you like.

2. Magazines with lots of pictures. Again you don't necessarily have to buy these, although if you want specific specialist subject areas covered, you may want to purchase magazines that are focussed on those areas. I have often found it cheapest to go to second hand book stores that also offer magazines, in that sort of place I have typically paid 50 pence or less for magazines. You can also go to libraries and ask if they have magazines they are throwing out. Ask the librarian to put them aside for you to collect every month, or once a quarter.

3. Scissors and glue. You will be cutting out the pictures and gluing them to your card, so you need sharp scissors. I have found that glue sticks are the best option for this exercise. They are the least messy and tend to hold firm for quite a long time.

4. Coloured fibre tip pens. I like to write and draw on my vision board as well as stick pictures onto it, so it's

handy to have coloured pens, or even paint if you are super-creative.

Once you have assembled all the necessary materials, the next step is to do a short visualisation to open your heart and mind. This allows you to expand your belief in the possibilities for your life and gets you into a more creative space. You might want to read through this visualisation and then close you eyes and take the journey, or you could read it aloud and record yourself so that you can listen and follow along.

Close your eyes and bring all your awareness to your breathing. Take three deep breaths and then allow yourself to settle into a slow, gentle rhythm that feels comfortable for you. Be present with your breath in your body. Now imagine that rather than your nose or mouth, you are actually breathing through your heart. Allow all your attention and focus to move to your physical heart and imagine breathing through that place in your chest.

With every breath, imagine your heart opening and expanding. Allow any blocks or limitations to fall away. Keep breathing slowly and steadily.

Next, move the focus of your breath to your mind. Imagine breathing in and out through your mind. With every breath allow your mind to expand.

Finally, start imagining your ideal life. With your mind and heart expanded, allow your imagination to grow great eagle wings and take flight. Be willing to become child-like, suspending reality for these few moments. Release all thoughts of 'what is' and allow yourself to imagine anything and everything you would love.

Imagine that you have all the time and all the money in the world. With these endless resources, what would you love to experience? Allow your imagineering to grow and expand into endless possibilities.

When you feel as though you have conjured up everything from your expanded imagination, then gradually bring your full awareness back to your breath, and when you are ready, open your eyes.

Now for the fun, easy bit. Thumb through the magazines. As you find pictures that represent or symbolise things that you imagined, cut them out and set them in a pile. This is a great opportunity for your inner five-year-old to come out and play. Get creative. I often cut out letters and make up words that have meaning. Or even find the exact word used in a totally different context. Allow this to be fun. If you have a family, get everyone playing. Get a group of like-minded friends together and play. Allow it to be fun, open, creative and expansive.

Once you have cut out all the pictures you want, you now get to stick them on your board. This is not a school homework assignment, it doesn't have to look a certain way. My boards are always all higgledy-piggledy, with pictures overlapping, everything at jaunty angles, with my hand-drawn pictures and writing to add meaning and context to the things I couldn't find represented in the magazines.

Try not to over-analyse the process. It really is as fun and simple as it sounds. Once you have completed your board to your own satisfaction, put it up somewhere. I have mine on the wall at the end of my bed, so that in the evenings and the mornings I can sit in bed and play games imagining the things I see coming into my life. This is a dynamic thing. It is meant to inspire you and allow you to see beyond everyday life, into that greatest yet to be that is calling you forward.

Belief Busting In Your Vocational Life

Chapter 12

WEALTHY BEYOND MEASURE
WITH EMPTY POCKETS

*"It is not the creation of wealth that is wrong,
but the love of money for its own sake."*

~ MARGARET THATCHER

Every time I teach a conscious creation class, there are two primary things people are seeking to create with this technology. They alternate in order of priority. One is the perfect mate and the other is more money. In this chapter we are going to unpick some of your beliefs about money. We are also going to delve deeper into the meanings and relevance of abundance, prosperity, and wealth.

Let us first look at the differing definitions of these three words:

Abundance: The Oxford Dictionary defines abundance as "a very large quantity of something", for example, "I have an abundance of cat hair on my carpet". It is possible to have an abundance of anything, for example: love, health, joy, sports socks and money. Beyond the dictionary definition, *abundance* is a feeling and a principle of *more than enough*. Similar to *wealthy*, *abundant* can be used to refer to a plentiful supply of something, and to an attitude of mind. One can live in a state of abundance regardless of any amount of material goods one may have accrued.

Wealth: The old definition of *wealth* is 'well-being',

particularly in relation to health. More commonly it is used to mean having lots of material goods, including money. It might also be used in a similar way to *abundance*, for example, "She has a *wealth* of knowledge." In this book I also use *wealth* and *wealthy* to refer to attitudes of mind or feelings of having more than enough of something that may not be tangible, such as a "*wealth* of love in my life."

Prosperity: Defined as "materially successful", *prosperity* is the manifestation of wealth and abundance. It is the demonstration of the principle of abundance by the acquisition of money, things and experience. It is also possible to develop a strong *prosperity* consciousness, that is to say, that you can live with a prosperous attitude beyond money and things.

In reading these definitions you may have your own opinion and possibly your own variation of meanings. Hopefully we are now all on the same page with regard to these important words and their usage in this chapter.

I am very blessed in my life. I consider myself to be wealthy beyond all measure. As you read this sentence, what does it mean to you? And what story are you making up about me?

Let me tell you what I mean when I say *I am wealthy beyond all measure*. Firstly, I do not measure wealth by a number in my bank account. Whilst I affirm that "I am a multimillionaire living in the constant flow of infinite opulence", I'm not quite there yet, and when I am, I will be no more or less wealthy than I am right now. Here are the things that I believe make me wealthy beyond all measure:

- I have a wonderful personal connection to my Source
- I have a loving, compassionate and utterly awesome life partner whom I adore
- I enjoy vibrant health, physically, mentally and emotionally

- I live a joy-filled, playful life
- I am surrounded by people who love me and accept me just as I am
- I have true friends all around the world who love and support me
- I get to do work and service that fills my heart with joy every day
- I have a loving family
- I have a safe roof over my head
- I have enough food to eat when I'm hungry
- The work and service I do makes a difference in people's lives
- I love and accept myself, just as I am, even on the bad days
- I belong to a global tribe of truth seekers and life lovers who are all working towards enabling one conscious humanity.

This list could also equally be the reasons I consider myself successful. How does this list resonate with you? Hopefully it is giving you the opportunity to rethink your definition of wealth.

The first item on my list is my connection to Source. You will notice that I have capitalised the 'S'. That is because I am referring to the God of my understanding. I have many names for that thing, of which Source is one. I believe in One Power or Consciousness or Mind. There are many names for that force and I don't think it matters in any way what you feel comfortable calling it/him/her. I encourage you to develop your own deeply personal connection to whatever you consider to be your Source.

The meaning of money

> *"Prosperity is a way of living and thinking, and not just money or things. Poverty is a way of living and*

thinking, and not just a lack of money or things."
~ ERIC BUTTERWORTH

Let us take a walk back in time and investigate the history of money. Money, in the form of shells and similar devices, only came into use around 2500 years ago. Prior to that the ancient system of *barter* had remained in place all around the world. However, money only became managed and controlled in the way it is today much more recently. To my simple mind, the only reason for moving from bartering to cash money is to make it easier to value and exchange the vast array of different goods and services which started to appear as human culture and society developed. In the early days of human existence the average person had only a few things they could swap, or barter. For one person perhaps that was goats' milk, herbs and firewood. Their neighbour had corn, straw and wheat. With just a few things available to trade it was easy to value different things in relation to each other. Think about all the things you pay for during an average day. How could you possibly barter for all of them on a daily basis? You'd never get anything exciting done.

When we think about money in modern times, it is simply a means of swapping two completely different things. It's a common denominator. There is no magic meaning that money is automatically imbued with. The physical coins or bits of paper which we use to symbolise particular amounts are largely worthless. The only meaning and value money has is what we give to it. That comes on an individual basis and a collective basis.

So what meaning do you give to money? Is it simply a means to an end? Is it the *'root of all evil'*, which, just to clarify, is a misinterpretation from the Christian Bible. The actual quote is the *"lust (or love) of money is the root of all evil"* (1 Timothy 6:10). Is money something that makes you feel safe when you look at the thousands in your bank account and fearful when there's less?

It is your beliefs about money that affect your experience with it; typically those beliefs are the ones that you learned and absorbed through your childhood. We'll dive deep into your money beliefs in the awareness exercise at the end of the chapter. But, just for now, what messages did you experience about money when you were growing up?

When I was a very small child I was not aware of money. I have no recollection of hearing my parents talk about it in any way. As I got a little older my family was affected by one of the first recessions in the post war era, which resulted in my father going to work in the Middle East for two years. That was when my conscious mind started to notice money and the cause and effect chain that surrounds having it or not having it. We never went without in the material world; Mum did an excellent job of managing the money. Whilst I'm sure balancing the household budget may have been stressful for her, as a child I was never aware of that stress. It is these kinds of events from childhood that can be very influential to the subconscious mind. Did you experience anything like this whilst you were growing up? Did you experience adults arguing about money when you were young, or did you experience extreme hardship growing up? Any of these experiences can have a significant impact on our money beliefs as an adult.

My understanding about the power of the mind and our beliefs has enabled me to liberate and release some of my old stories about money, wealth and abundance. There are always more layers of the onion to peel, and occasionally I will hear myself say something from my old programming. I'm quite good at catching myself, and I have people around me who will very lovingly call me out when something unwanted tumbles from my mouth.

An example of this happened just the other day. I was busy in a conversation about abundance and prosperity and I found myself saying something about the 'difficult economic climate that exists at the moment'. I caught myself and mentally rewired my conversation to witness the *appearance* of a difficult economic climate. That appearance only comes true for me if I believe it and put my attention, energy and focus on it.

I know it is possible that you are reading this and thinking, "It *is* a difficult economic climate." My invitation to you is to open a space within your mind to the possibility that the economic climate is neither difficult or easy, like weather, it simply is what it is. The more we, as a collective humanity, put our attention, energy and focus on what we want, rather than what we are told is *true,* the sooner we will step into a more thriving world. Letting go of what is or has always been, and focussing on what you want to experience, in any area of your life, is one way to ignite success beyond beliefs and create a thriving life beyond your current experience.

Letting go is essential to growth

> *"If you always do what you've always done,*
> *you'll always get what you've always got."*

In researching this quote, I find it is attributed to Henry Ford, Tony Robbins and about three other people. Whoever said it first, I'm grateful and I honour and acknowledge their wisdom. What is it you keep doing in your financial life, yet expecting to get a different result?

If you want to have a different experience of money and abundance, you may want to adopt different beliefs, take different actions, and develop new habits. Money has no worth, value or meaning other than that we give it. Money is a means of circulating energy in much the same way as an electrical circuit moves energy around your home. Just like a power station, you do certain things and take certain actions to create the energy (money), such as going to work, delivering a service, or making a product. You sell your time, service or product for a certain amount of money, which gives you energy in your store.

You know that if you want to use the power created in a power station you need to plug a device into a socket and flick the switch. Assuming that your home is connected to some form of mains supply or generator, your electrical device will start working and you will be spending your energy. The energy of your money is no different. You have specific places where you spend your money, such as the rent, the hairdresser, the car, the supermarket, etc. Just like the electrical circuit, you are in the circular flow of receiving money in and spending it out. This flow is healthy. Flow, in all things, is the essence of the natural world. I don't expect you give much thought to electricity if you are living in the first world. Money is no different, yet we give it an inordinate amount of attention.

I have some very early memories from the 1970s in England when there were miners' strikes and what was called the 'three day week' was imposed. Power station workers could only work three days a week due to the lack of coal. During that time there would be power cuts in the evening because there wasn't enough energy in the country's tanks. For a little girl who loved fire, I was delighted because we had to light candles in the sitting room and I could get lost in the magic of watching the flames flicker and jump. However I'm sure it was a challenge for the adults who had to arrange baths for grubby children, make lunches and get other work done without electricity. If that happened today I'm not sure many people would know what to do with themselves without the electronic gadgets we so rely on. Go back to watching the candles flicker, I guess.

Sometimes the same thing can happen with our financial situation. The flow stops. Like the power cuts, it may stop because of a lost job or illness. It may also stop because of fear that there may not be enough in the future. In all things, fear acts to limit flow. When we become fearful in any situation our breathing constricts, and sometimes stops completely; the flow of air reduces or stops. No matter what the cause, if the in and out of circulation stops at either end, there's a problem. Imagine a dam where water keeps coming in, but none is released. Eventually, at the very least it will overflow; worst-case could result in the increased pressure breaking through the dam and flooding the valley below. Neither is a desirable outcome, which is why most dams have control valves to manage water levels and maintain the flow.

Whilst I'm no financial advisor, it's probably common sense to have a dam for some of your money, to save a little. But if saving is a consuming priority with no specific goal in mind, you may want to check in with what you believe about the flow of money in your life. I have met several people for whom a hidden fear of becoming destitute has caused them to squeeze all the joy out of life and to hoard everything they get. That kind of fear is eventually going to create a situation like the example of the dam. Something in your life will overflow or burst because you are not living in the flow. In my experience with clients, this kind of money fear often overflows in the form of panic attacks, anxiety, stress or depression.

What feelings are you experiencing as you read this conversation about money? I once heard another coach say that it was easier for many of her clients to talk about their sex lives than it was to talk about their money. Is all this talk of money causing you to feel uncomfortable? Is it one aspect or element of money, or the entire money subject that causes discomfort? Whichever it is, simply make a mental note, or jot it in your journal. You will find it useful in the awareness exercise at the end.

Rich or poor, it's more than cash

> *"Conditions or circumstances, such as mates, jobs,*
> *currency, numbers on computer screens and 'things out*
> *there', do not cause your* (money) *experience."*
> ~ KAREN RUSSO, *THE MONEY KEYS*

Would you rather feel prosperous or poor? This may seem like a strange question to ask and you may assume that everyone will say 'prosperous', but that may not be the case. I have worked with clients for whom the idea of prosperity was, initially, so linked with the burdensome responsibility of managing money that they would select poverty every time. Is it possible that you may have a similar belief lurking somewhere in your subconscious?

Remember, the subconscious mind holds all kinds of beliefs hidden from sight. The best way to recognise any hidden beliefs you have concerning abundance, prosperity, money and wealth is to look at your situation. If you feel affluent, prosperous and wealthy; if you have a consistent flow of physical money; if you feel confident and comfortable talking about money, then you probably don't have any significant hidden beliefs. If, on the other hand, you feel poor, have debt, and fear money conversations, it is far more likely that you have hidden beliefs about money.

Take a moment to get quiet in your mind and complete this sentence, "Money is......"

You could take the time to complete this sentence several times if you have lots of words and phrases that come up. Allow yourself the opportunity to go a little deeper. You may even want to close your eyes and sit with the question. You might be surprised at what reveals from within you. Often when clients do this exercise, they are totally unaware of the beliefs that are hiding inside their minds.

The awareness exercises we do throughout this book are designed to allow hidden beliefs to bubble to the surface. Once they become apparent we can start to deal with them. There are different ways to counter beliefs that you want to change and reprogram. Let's take an earlier example, it's one that I was raised with and have lots of experience resolving.

Money is...... the root of all evil.

Here are some steps to counter, reverse and reprogram beliefs:

1. Logical argument

Firstly, as I already mentioned, this is a mis-quote. The Bible says that, *"the lust for money is the root of all evil."* Which is something we can all probably agree on. If we were all to live a life focussed solely on the acquisition of wealth, to constantly lust for money, the world would be a poorer place.

We have already discussed the idea that money itself is simply energy. The metal and paper that money is created from is worthless. The value is something we agree on and, as we know from the money markets and banking crises, the value can change overnight. Money can only be evil if we believe it is. Such a belief does not support my intention and dream for my life, so I'm letting it go.

2. Affirmations

Flip your belief around and create positive affirmations from it. In this case here are some possibilities:

Money is neutral.

I make up my own meaning about money.

Money is the energy of love in constant flow through my life.

Money is a common denominator.

Money allows different things to be exchanged easily around the world.

Money makes my life easy.

3. Creative visualisation

The image created by the sentence, "Money is the root of all evil", is not a positive one. Use the affirmations above to inspire new, positive images of money. Imagine yourself in the scenes enjoying money, circulating money freely, creating new delightful experiences in your mind.

Remember to use all your physical senses as you imagine this new reality.

These three steps can be used over and over again with every belief you discover. They don't even have to be the hidden beliefs. You can use this same process to reprogram your mind from any belief that you want to change. Although it is possible for you to complete these steps once and completely change your belief, it is more likely that you will need to repeat them regularly. This is particularly true for steps 2 and 3. Say your affirmations over and over again. Spend time regularly visualising or imagining your new reality. Our brain is one of habit, and creating a new habit takes 21 days, so you probably want to make time every day, for at least 21 days, to practise these new habits.

Feeling wealthy no matter what

> *"Feeling is the secret."*
>
> ~ NEVILLE GODDARD

This quote is also a book title from Neville Goddard. It is widely available and I heartily recommend you read it. In this powerful little book Neville guides us, with his own wisdom, and with many tales from his students and clients, into the powerful use of our imagination. As the title suggests, his focus is on creating the physical and emotional feelings as part of our imagined world. So how do you feel wealthy when there is nothing in your pockets and the cupboards are bare?

Empty pockets and cupboards can reasonably create some fear, as well as shame and possibly guilt. Just to clarify, there is a difference between guilt and shame. Guilt is the feeling that you have done something wrong, whereas shame is the feeling that you are wrong. It may also be interpreted as the feeling of not being enough. As I have experienced in my own life, when we feel we are not enough in any area of life, it becomes difficult to create abundance and prosperity. To the best of your ability look for the things that you do have in abundance and celebrate them. Also look around you in nature or the city and become more aware of the demonstrations of abundance that surround you. Depending on the time of year, and where you live, there may be an abundance of blossom, daffodils, sunshine, autumn leaves, snow, sand, migrating birds or whales, freshly mown grass and lots of other things.

As we get deeper into the feeling of appreciation and thankfulness we can move further toward creating a physical shift in our situation. If you are struggling financially I invite you to spend some time separating the feelings and beliefs from the facts. When I experienced financial hardship I found that most of the stress came from the stories I was making up. When I got clear on the facts, and took the practical action I could to resolve the situation, things became much easier. Do the best you can to focus on the good you have in your life, no matter how little it may appear, and move your attention away from any feelings of fear and shame. You are born from the principle of success, you are worthy and deserving of a fabulous life, no matter what your current situation may be.

You are enough and you have enough

Having read this far into the chapter, my hope is that you are already moving beyond the 'money = wealth' equation. Thinking about your life, what good things do you already have an abundance of? Is it friends, family, love, fun, playfulness, good health, books, time, talents, music? In my life I would add books and music to my list of abundance. I am looking forward to having a home with a room dedicated to books and music so that I can have them all in one place. You may want to look back at the beginning of this chapter and refer to my list of reasons I feel wealthy. That may inspire you to add some more items to your list.

Another reference point for abundance which I regularly reflect on is the abundance in nature. Depending on the time of year, I see an abundance of leaves, blossom, fruit, wheat, yellow, green, brown. I live on the coast, the beach has pebbles with very little sand, so I can always imagine an abundance of pebbles. Sand is another great example of nature's abundance. Just try and imagine all the grains of sand that exist on the planet. Even if you imagined picking up a scoop of sand in your cupped hands you would probably struggle to count all the individual grains. Nature is abundant, and it operates in the natural flow, always giving and receiving.

My favourite example of this cycle of life is the cherry tree outside my office window. In the spring it bursts forth with fresh leaves and flowers. The flowers move through their life cycle. The bees and other insects buzz and flutter around, enjoying the feast and pollinating as they go. Then the warm spring breeze gets a little lively and the blossom is scattered all around the path and road. As we roll into summer the cherry fruit ripens and now it is the birds' turn to feast. The fruit gets eaten and the cherry stones fall to the ground, ready to seed a new generation of cherry trees. Some stones find fertile soil and others get crushed beneath car tyres. Eventually, as autumn brings the crisp air and threatens the dark and damp of winter, the leaves turn brown and fall to the earth as the tree gets ready to take a sleep for the winter.

During this cycle there is no point at which the tree thinks to itself, "Hmm, I might not have enough energy later, perhaps I should hang on to these beautiful blossoms, these luscious fruit or these verdant leaves." The tree knows and trusts the cycle of life. The natural process of change, of ebb and flow is what allows the tree to grow and expand and to live a thriving life. We have much to learn from the wisdom of trees and of nature in general.

Change is essential to all life and to all growth. The universal imperative of *grow or die* is true in every aspect of life. If you really want to ignite success beyond your beliefs, embracing change as your new best friend is one of the most useful things you can do. Just like a caterpillar transforming into a butterfly, sometimes change can feel incredibly uncomfortable, yet it's still essential for our conscious growth.

As you breathe into this new understanding, are you beginning to feel more able to recognise your own wealth and abundance? Are you appreciating that money is a function of life and has very little to do with feeling wealthy or abundant? Once again, take a breath and think about all that you already have in your life. There is great power in feeling and expressing gratitude. Just for a few moments, allow yourself to really feel grateful for all that you have.

You are a money magnet

"Money won't create success, the freedom to make it will."

~ NELSON MANDELA

Changing your mind about the meaning of money does not necessarily change the everyday requirement to have some. Living in the developed world there is a very practical need for cash to live. Now we have looked at work and money with fresh eyes, let us think about our ability to create change in our physical money situation.

Discovering what we really think about money, by asking different questions and becoming more aware of our physical circumstance, we have realised where some of our blocks and limits might be. We have looked at a three step process - logical argument; affirmations; visualisation - to counter and reprogram specific beliefs. In addition we have found ways to recognise and embrace our own wealth, abundance and prosperity without reference to money.

These steps may appear to be separate and disconnected; actually they are all working collaboratively within you to rewire your money mind and to open up new possibilities. With a change of mind already happening, it's time to return to money and ask some new questions:

1. What's the money for?
2. Are you open to receive?
3. What do you believe about your source?
4. What do you believe you deserve?

Let's look at these questions one at a time.

Question 1: What's the money for?

Often we get stuck in the idea that we need X amount of money to get Y. Just as an example, I need £500 to buy a Vitamix blender. On the surface that is true. But there's another way of looking at this. When I change my thought to, 'I would love to have a Vitamix blender', I release the specific need for £500 and instead use the tools I already know to invite the infinite imagination of the Universe to deliver a Vitamix into my life.

My friend Terry was gifted a Vitamix by a happy client. My friend Leanne found one on a late night shopping channel, super cheap, and with a payment plan. Costco, a well known US wholesaler who recently opened up in the UK, typically sells them at a much lower price that other retail outlets. There is an endless array of possibilities when I open my mind and imagination beyond the money. When we get bogged down in a single belief about what is possible, we are limiting the Universe. When we look beyond the money, the infinite once again becomes visible to us.

Question 2: Are you open to receive?

Staying with my Vitamix example, if someone were to gift me a £500 Vitamix would I be comfortable receiving it? This is a really good question to ask yourself. Many people can't even receive a free compliment about their clothes without feeling the need to pass it off with a comment like, "This old thing?", or "It was a bargain in a charity shop." If you can't receive a nice comment about your clothes, how will you ever receive a gift worth £500?

I had a great lesson in giving and the ability to receive a few years back. A friend of mine really wanted a Land Rover (the English version of a Jeep). He'd been in the army and had some mobility issues, and thought that a Land Rover would be the perfect vehicle for him. He didn't have much money at the time, and was doing the best he could to get his life in order. As chance would have it, I came into some unexpected money, so I bought him a Land Rover. We went off and checked it out. It was old, but functional, so I bought it for him, no strings attached, just a gift.

He was super excited, like a kid in a candy store, totally delighted with his new vehicle. Yet, within six weeks, he had wrecked it and needed to pay for it to be towed to a garage. He was never able to have it fixed because he didn't have the money to pay for the repairs. Although I didn't know it at the time, I now see clearly that he wasn't open to receive. In addition, subconsciously he didn't believe he deserved to have his own Land Rover. Check in with yourself, is there an upper limit on the value of something you would be willing to receive? Could you receive a valuable gift without having the need to match the value in a gift back to the giver?

If you are not willing to receive without the need to deflect or give back, why not? What story have you learned about receiving? Does it mean you are in some way beholden to the giver? Does it mean that you are 'less than' in some way if you can't reciprocate? This is another one of those important areas of belief that is valuable to delve into. After all, if you are not willing to receive, how will you ever create a thriving, abundant life? Life is a constant flow, remember, and just like the tide, that flow comes and goes.

Question 3: What do you believe about your source?

Where does your money and your good come from? Are you limited to believing that your source is a job, a spouse, a parent, an inheritance or some other specific person or situation? Initially you may say, 'Yes!' to this question. I invite you expand your belief and allow the Infinite Universe to be your source. When you open a space within your belief system that says, "My good can come from anywhere and anyone", you are once again opening a fresh space for all good things to come to you. Here is another great affirmation to help open that space in your mind:

I now accept my good from expected and unexpected sources.

Gifts, tax rebates, competition winnings and lottery jackpots are all examples of unexpected sources. If your inner chatter is saying something like, "right, like I could win the lottery or get a tax rebate" as you read this, that's a clue to let you know you have more opportunities for growth and learning when it comes to unpicking your money mind. Allow this new awareness, without judgement, then get to work on investigating what you believe.

Question 4: What do you believe you deserve?

In my experience, worthiness and deservability are key human issues in the developed world. Paradoxically, we have so much physical 'stuff', yet the vast majority of us have deep-seated insecurities around our basic worth. I know I have already mentioned this, but it certainly bears another mention.

You are enough, you came into this physical suitcase being enough, you will eventually leave it behind, and you will still be enough. Your worth is not dependent on what or how much you produce; how much (or little) academic education you have; the amount of money in your bank account; the number of 'friends' you have on Facebook; the car you drive; the holidays you go on; or any other external measure you may think up.

Your worth is equal to, and yet unique from, that of every other being on the planet. You are worthy and deserving simply because you breathe, and you showed up. You are worthy no matter what anyone ever told you, how they treated you, or what you have done. And whilst I can keep telling you this until I'm blue in the face, it is only as you allow yourself to embrace and embody your worth as your personal truth that you will be able to quiet the chattering voice in your head telling you otherwise.

Breathe deep, repeat to yourself, out loud, "I am enough, I am enough, I am enough". Close your eyes and keep repeating. Make a mental note of any argument your chatter voice comes up with. Do your best to keep repeating, "I am enough". Avoid getting into dialogue with the chatter voice, this is one of those occasions when negotiation isn't the aim. That can come later. As you keep repeating, aloud, "I am enough", connect into your body, notice as it starts to feel a little more true.

How long and how often you need to keep repeating this affirmation for it to sink in will depend on how far away you are from believing it when you start. This is another one of those occasions when it is necessary to apply the 3Ps of practise, persistence and patience. I will continue to know the truth of you as complete and perfectly whole whilst you do the practise to embody this truth for yourself.

As you open and expand your belief in your worth, you will also be opening and expanding your ability to receive good, in all its forms, into your life. If a core belief in your subconscious mind is, "I am not worthy", then on a very subtle level you will not allow good into your life. As that changes and you rewire your mind, you will see the results change and the flow of everything good will increase.

It's already all yours

Everything you could ever want is already yours. I don't believe there is anything beyond you and your subconscious mind's preventing you from having your heart's desire. Even if this is something you have been told is impossible, such as full recovery from a difficult diagnosis, I believe it is possible for you to experience it. Whether you do or don't achieve or receive your heart's desire is down to you. Are you willing to do new things, think differently and open up to changing your mental and physical habits?

Whether or not you achieve your dreams, you are still wealthy beyond measure. You are still worthy and deserving of living your dream life. Another one of those weird paradoxes: once you believe these things, you are already living your dreams, appreciating your wealth, and embodying your worth even though nothing in the physical realm has changed yet. This is because you have stepped into the embodiment of the principles of success and abundance. When you realise that who you really are and that your essential wellbeing are not affected by anything outside of you, that is when you are able to stay in peace, happiness, prosperity and love, regardless of external circumstances.

I know it's possible to get there because I have done it in my own life. I live a relatively modest life in material terms, but I am overflowing with joy, vibrancy, abundance, health and wealth. I appreciate everything that comes and goes in my life as part of the journey. I truly feel very blessed and eternally grateful for all that I have in my life. Trust me, if I can do it, anyone can.

Chapter 12 - Awareness exercise - Discovering what you really believe

I really value self enquiry as a personal discovery tool. I invite you to take a breath and connect with your heart. Do your best to answer these questions from a place beyond your conscious mind. Endeavour not to put the answers you'd like to believe, but the true thoughts that are bubbling up from your chatter mind. It is only when you can reveal some of these hidden beliefs that you can use all the other tools to flip them.

As you delve deeper into these questions please consider consulting with a qualified professional if you experience strong emotion.

When I hear a conversation about money I feel _____

_____

_____

_____

When it comes to managing my money I feel _____

_____

_____

_____

Money is _____

_____

_____

_____

When it comes to money I believe I deserve _____

_____

_____

When it comes to money I believe I don't deserve _____

_____

As you complete these sentences and discover the things you want to change, use the 3 step process of argument, affirmations and visualisation (detailed above) to change your beliefs and thinking.

You may also want to take these sentences into your meditation or contemplation practice to see what else reveals to you.

Always remember: you are already wealthy beyond measure.

Wealthy Beyond Measure With Empty Pockets

Chapter 13

WHAT'S GOD GOT TO DO WITH IT?

"The eye through which I see God is the same eye through which God sees me; my eye and God's eye are one eye, one seeing, one knowing, one love."

~ MEISTER ECKHART

For many people the word 'God' is so loaded that it acts to block any kind of growth and learning. Depending on your belief system you are already engaged or disengaged with this chapter just from reading the title and the quote above. Which are you, and why? Let me take a moment to explain what I mean when I use the word 'God'. And, what I don't mean.

For me, God is a word I use to mean the wholeness of life and unconditional love. I believe there is a power far greater than I, in my individual self, am. I believe it is the life force in everything from you and me to the rocks and the oceans. Quantum scientists call this same thing 'light' or 'energy'. You might call it Universe, Spirit, Source, Allah, Consciousness, All In All, Everything, Yahweh, Nothing, The Way, Light, Non-duality, Vishnu, Universal Mind, or my personal favourite - Love.

I do not seek to change your religious or faith-based belief system, but I am inviting you to consider why you believe what you believe and to contemplate how those beliefs support your expanded vision for your life. For me, God is not a middle-aged white guy sitting on a cloud, with a long beard, judging my every move and keeping score of my worth. It's great if that idea works for you. But it simply doesn't resonate with me. I have studied many of the world's religions and philosophies, both ancient and more recent, and I have been meditating for over 30 years. Between my study and my personal connection to the Infinite, I have developed a very personal relationship to the One that works for me. My best invitation to you is that you also seek your own connection and build your personal relationship to the God of your understanding.

The Meister Eckhart quote at the beginning of the chapter speaks well to the God of my understanding. I see, sense, feel and know one thing, not two things. I am not separate from that power, I am also not separate from you. As the Quantum theorists will tell us, everything is one thing. Everything is energy. That energy can be harnessed in individual things and used in different ways, but there is no difference between the energy producing electric light and the energy creating gas-fired heat. You and I, and the other seven plus billion people on the planet, are all here in our individualised human suitcases, our own energetic expressions. Each unique and perfect in physical form, but the energy that impels us is the same energy.

We are one, you and I. We are also one with all the birds, animals, insects, fish, rocks, trees, grass, water and everything else that exists. If we look at the ancient indigenous people in many locations globally, this is the truth they have always known. In our modern, technology-driven world, many people, particularly in the developed world, have lost their connection to their Source. For me, reconnecting to that which is both in me and around me has enabled a level of growth, compassion and deep love to become my permanent inner fuel. It is something that can never be taken away. This is one way that we can ignite success beyond beliefs and step into a greater experience of life.

One of the few things that I remember from my high school

science class is that energy cannot be created or destroyed. It changes form, but never disappears. That is what I believe about us, and every other life force. Our energy exists always. We come into this particular body suitcase, and we have our grand adventure travelling through this thing we call 'life'. Once we get done, we hop out, leaving the carbon suitcase behind, and return to wherever we came from. That's what I believe. I'm not saying I'm right or wrong, nor do I seek your agreement or conformity, it's just what works for me. What do you believe? It's valuable to get clear about what you believe because your beliefs will shape your life experience.

> *"Love is God, and to die means that I, a particle of love, shall return to the general and eternal source."*
>
> ~ LEO TOLSTOY

Let me also take a moment to talk about what I mean when I use the term 'unconditional love'. There is a compassionate love which is more than the flutter of excitement we feel at the beginning of a new romantic relationship. It is deeper than the love we feel at the arrival of a new child. It goes beyond all judgement, all expectation, all behaviour. It is a love that says, 'no matter who you are, or what you do, or where you have come from, there is nothing you can do that could make me love you more and there is nothing you can do that could make me love you less.' It is a love which recognises the true essence of every being and connects to that place of love within us. Rumi put it thus, "Beyond right doing and wrong doing there is a field, I will meet you there." As we each awaken to that deep well of loving compassion within us, we can more easily seek, and find it, in all that we meet.

Spiritually conscious, not religious

I also believe there is a significant difference between being religious and being spiritually conscious. To me, religion speaks to rules, conformity, constriction, being right or wrong, and having the only way. Spirituality speaks to a personal connection, expansion, personal experience, fluidity, and all ways. The two are not mutually exclusive. I have met many religious people with a deep spirituality and an openness to other paths.

I was notionally raised in the Church of England, which is a protestant-based Christian faith. I went to a Church-run school until I was eleven. The vicar regularly came to school and spoke at morning assembly; the entire school would form a crocodile line and walk through the village to the church for significant events in the calendar. I also attended Crusaders, a Sunday school held in the village hall.

I use the term 'notionally' at the beginning of the previous paragraph because although I had all this great education in the teachings of the New Testament, it didn't really rub off on me. My Mum would describe herself as a Christian, but didn't go to church regularly. My Dad always described himself as a student of Buddhism, particularly Zen Buddhism, although as a child he was raised in the Dutch Reformed Church in South Africa. With all these different influences, I have come to realise that I was a seeker from a very young age. Thinking about your childhood, what influenced you in matters of faith, spirituality and religion? How have those influences impacted your beliefs today?

Spirituality, a feeling of connection to something more than you are, has been shown to improve psychological states. It doesn't seem to matter what your particular faith or philosophy is, simply that the belief in a higher power of some form generally makes you more emotionally resilient, and statistically generates better physical and mental health. Research suggests that having faith, of any kind, provides a coping mechanism for life's ups and downs. In my own experience, my faith enables me to have greater trust in the process of life, which in turn, provides greater patience and confidence when things don't appear to be going the way I want them to go.

Mental and emotional resilience are valuable skills to build along our journey. They allow us to weather the storm of life's challenging events. No matter what your faith, or lack of it, what beliefs do you have about yourself and the world around you when things don't go the way you want them to? Life happens. It is often difficult to see that when things go wrong it's not a test or a punishment, it's just life happening. It happens equally to us all. How we are able to process undesirable events when they happen is dependent on our beliefs and our experiences. What kind of stories do you make up when something happens in your life which you would rather not experience? Do you blame yourself? Do you feel you are being 'done to' by an external force? Do you seek reasons to blame 'them'; the other people involved in the situation? Instead of looking for the negative answer to get relief, could you ask yourself, "Why is this happening *for* me?" When you shift your perspective around, let go of blaming and shaming, others or yourself, and open to the possibility that even the challenges are happening *for* you, *if* you are willing to look for it, for your good and expansion, it really brings a sense of relief and allows another opening for your good to reveal.

You are not alone

"Smile, breathe and go slowly."

~ THICH NHAT HANH

When we discover our own, deeply personal, connection with Source, it allows us to feel as though we have been enveloped in an experience of love deeper and wider than we can possibly articulate with words. We feel a sense of connection to life, in all its forms, which fills us with strength and confidence. It brings a knowing, no matter what we experience in our everyday life, that we are never alone. We feel the indwelling presence of the Divine deep at our core. There are still times when we don't remember the connection, when

219

we feel separate, but those moments become fewer and the process of remembering gets faster. How would your life be different if you truly knew you were loved and looked after? If you felt connected, inside and out, to a powerful force for good that was always with you? Igniting success beyond beliefs is much easier to do when you feel a deep sense of connection to something more than you are. That is why it is valuable to get clear about your personal spiritual beliefs.

Like everything else we have talked about, igniting success and building new beliefs around your connection to Life is about evaluating the beliefs you already have and making objective, non-judgmental decisions about how they serve you. If you were raised in a strong faith tradition this may be very difficult to do. You will probably fall into one of two camps - you will either reject everything to do with faith or spiritual connection, or you will be deeply invested in your teachings from childhood. Either way, if you are looking for a deeper sense of connection and support in your life, perhaps it's time to take a look at what you believe and why.

In the UK I have found that the most divisive word in spiritual and faith communities is the 'G' word: God. Depending on where you live now and where you were raised, just like the different housing types we talked about at the beginning of the book, you will have different beliefs and meanings attached to the word 'god'. You may also use a multitude of other words that have a similar feeling tone to them. I once read that there are over 2500 words that refer to a higher power. When I teach, I tell my students that with so many diverse words available, it is probable that they will be able to find at least one that feels right to them. I give you the same invitation. We have already discussed the importance of *feeling* the vision and the words. This is no different - find words that you can connect to, and which resonate through your body.

Take a breath and check in with these sentences, take a moment to complete them in your mind:

When I hear the word 'god', I feel ....
When I hear people speak about god I think ....
If I speak about god I'm speaking about ....

Depending on your beliefs, you may have an opinion about the absence of a capital 'G' at the beginning of 'God'. It is often in these subtle thoughts and reactions that we can discover our deeper, frequently hidden, beliefs. Take a moment to check-in with yourself. Did you feel a sense of irritation or offence at seeing God spelled as god? It was a very deliberate intention on my part. My invitation to you is that you become better at noticing the things that pull your triggers. Through awareness comes the ability to change if you choose.

As with everything that has gone before in these chapters, become aware of your beliefs and then decide, "Is that supporting me and my intentions for my life, or not?" My dear friend Michael says he uses 'God' because it's the biggest word he knows. Rather than just reacting to certain words or phrases, now is the time to start observing, from a non-judgmental place, and allowing the light of awareness to inform your direction for growth.

> *"Christian, Jew, Muslim, shaman, Zoroastrian, stone,*
> *ground, mountain, river, each has a secret way of being with*
> *the mystery, unique and not to be judged"*
>
> ~ RUMI

In the Tao Te Ching it says, "The way that can be named is not the Great Way." In truth whenever we try to name the infinite we are taking away its very essence and nature. We are turning that infinite, unlimited thing into something which is finite and limited so that our small human minds can create understanding as well as division and ownership. It is time for us to move beyond the idea of separateness and remember our innate wholeness; everything is the one energy expressed in its own unique way.

Being different, individual and unique does not make us separate. To paraphrase the beloved poet and sage Rumi, from the quote above, each thing, be it Christian, Jew, Muslim, shaman, Zoroastrian, stone, ground, mountain, river, four legged, two legged, crawler or flyer, it is a unique and perfect expression of the one energy. It is our uniqueness that connects us. This is the way of nature. Perfectly you and always walking your individual path as a unique expression of the One energy. That is the truth of you.

We are to Life as a drop of water is to the ocean. Just as every drop of water is its own drop, it is everything that the ocean is, but one drop does not make the ocean. We are all that Life is, but each one of us comes together to make up all of life. Which is why your presence in this Life is essential to completing all of creation. Just as the ocean would be different if there were fewer drops, Life would be different if we were not here, expressing our uniqueness in this experience.

These ideas may challenge your current belief system, or they may not. My invitation is for you to notice what is happening in your mind. It's all about awareness. Do you find yourself having a strong opinion in one way or another? Or are you allowing these ideas to wash over you whilst you run them through your existing filters about how life is? Remember whatever thoughts are coming up are neither good nor bad, right nor wrong. This is an opportunity to become more aware of what you think and believe. As your awareness grows, you can review what works and what doesn't, so that you can start to gently release the things you are willing to change and embrace new supporting beliefs.

An empty well cannot quench anyone's thirst

My vision for you is that you discover your true Self and in that discovery you reveal new ways of being which enable and empower you into a life of self acceptance, self compassion, self belief and self confidence. The first appearance of these statements may be that this way of living is "selfish." In truth it is self-care. It has been my experience that when we truly can love and accept ourselves as we are, with all our human frailties, apparent faults and wrong thinking, then we become vastly more compassionate, non-judgmental and giving to all the beings we share our lives and our planet with.

Imagine living a life where you almost always feel like giving yourself from 'I'd love to' and not from 'I should'. A life in which you say, 'No' when you mean it, and don't feel guilty; always remembering that, 'No' is a complete sentence. Can you imagine a life where you feel your connection to all of Creation, and when you look in the mirror you feel a deep sense of love and compassion for all that you are? To get started can you imagine looking in the mirror and being okay with what you see?

No judgement - remember, you are where you are, and that's perfectly okay. With each new awareness, you have fresh choices to change your beliefs, habits and actions. As you make those new choices you will start to see changes happening in your life. You will be building your personal collection of evidence that will create a new upward spiral of success which in turn will inspire you to make new choices and experience more success and so it goes on.

Deepening your spiritual awareness

> *"All major religious traditions carry basically the same*
> *message, that is love, compassion and forgiveness ... the*
> *important thing is they should be part of our daily lives."*
>
> ~ DALAI LAMA

As we make each new choice and it informs our new habits, there is a growing desire to maintain the good feelings. That maintenance is a practice. In order to deepen your personal connection with the indwelling presence of the God of your understanding (Life, Source, Spirit, Love), you will be best served by the creation of spiritual practices that inspire and support you. There are some common elements for many people, and it is still your personal practice. You get to create whatever works for you.

My personal practice starts with writing, followed by around 30 minutes of mindfulness meditation in silence. I have a range of other practices that I use on different occasions in my life. All the tools I use in my own life are the same ones that I teach in all my work, including this book.

I find that my day works much better when I start with my meditation practice, once I finish writing. It centres me and grounds me back into the love and compassion at the core of my being. I reconnect to the indwelling presence of the divine through my practice. If you are seeking to know yourself more deeply and to reconnect with your own innate wholeness, mindful meditation is a great tool. It is the practice of allowing your mind to go where it will without diving into the stories. And it is a practice. If you have never taken much time to quiet your mind and sit still, you may be well advised to start with a short time, three or five minutes, set the egg timer or the timer on your phone. Sit still, without disturbances, and breathe. Allow your mind to wander and notice it's wandering without judgement. I always imagine the thoughts going by like clouds on a windy day. I don't need to get stuck in any particular one, they can just blow past.

With more practise it becomes easier and easier to quiet the mind and reconnect to Source. I have been meditating, in one form or another, for over thirty years, and there are still days when I find it almost impossible to stop the chattering monkey mind, so be gentle with yourself and build your practice slowly. It gets easier when you are consistent and persistent.

Another way I connect to the wholeness of Life is through nature. Walking, at the beach or in the woods, watching the birds swoop and dive, delighting in the spectacular display of a sunset, any of these things remind me that I am a drop in the ocean of life and that I am connected to all that I see. Take a breath. What reminds you to reconnect to Life?

Something within us, perhaps the feeling of divine discontent or perhaps the universal imperative of *grow or die,* calls us to seek something more. We try to fill that seeking with 'stuff': money, clothes, houses, cars, holidays, lovers, alcohol, drugs, gambling, food, sports, promotions, work and all the other things we use to numb the underlying feeling of dissatisfaction. I believe what we are really seeking is to reconnect with our Divine Essence. In truth, we can never be separate from it, but as humans, we sometimes forget.

The Random Accident

Once upon a time, a long time ago, there was a great monastery set high in the hills. The monastery was led by a great master, a very old wise monk, who had lived there for as long as he could remember. Because his reputation had spread far and wide many students and seekers came to the monastery to learn self mastery and the path to enlightenment.

Every day the master would school his students on the pathway to enlightenment. He would have them kneel and pray 10,000 times in each direction, east, south, west and north. He would make them sit in silent meditation hour after hour, admonishing them if they wriggled or moved even a twitch. He would have them walk and chant and ring the bells for all the other hours of the day. The students hardly had time to eat and slept a few short hours every night.

One day the great master decided to go to the village to share his teachings with the local people, whilst some of his students collected supplies for the monastery. Amongst the students that travelled down the mountain was a most attentive and bright young man who listened carefully to everything the master had to say. He never missed a syllable and was always incredibly diligent with his daily practice.

In the village a crowd had gathered, keenly awaiting the words of wisdom from the old monk. The bright young student sat quietly with the master, ensuring his comfort and needs were met. The master addressed the villagers with wise words. He told them of the importance of living a life of compassion and love, he spoke to them of treating their animals with the same care as they would their children. He spoke about the benefits of education and avoiding gluttony and greed. Then, just as the students were starting to gather with arms laden full of food and other essentials, the wise old master, concluding his lecture, said to the villagers, "enlightenment is really just a random accident."

The bright young student, who never missed a word the master spoke, was immediately puzzled and confused by the master's final statement. 'Enlightenment is really just a random accident.' "How can that be true?" thought the young man to himself. Ever the diligent student, he started to ponder on the long walk back up the mountain. He wondered if he had somehow missed something important the master had taught. Then he thought perhaps he had misheard what the master had actually said to the villagers. All in all, as he walked back to the monastery, the young man considered every possibility and was still utterly confused by what the master had said.

Eventually, plucking up the courage to ask his question, just as they got to the doors of the monastery, the young student spoke to the master. "Master, down in the village, you told the people that enlightenment is really just a random accident." "Yes," said the master, "I did." "Well," the student continued, "if that is the case, why do you make us do our 10,000 prayers in every direction, why do we sit for so long in silent meditation and how does ringing all those bells bring us enlightenment?"

Hearing this question the old monk smiled a knowing smile. He looked at the bright young man with great compassion and patience. With peace and wisdom that come from deep knowledge, the great master finally responded, "We do all our practice so that we may become more accident prone."

Perhaps the enlightenment we seek is our connection to Source and richer levels of self acceptance. No matter what we seek, it is in the practise that we open a wider space to experience something more than our individual expression of life.

Although our Divinity is the very core of who we are, as the story illustrates, remembering and living from that place within us needs practise. In seeking to consciously connect with our Divine Essence, it is valuable to spend time *being* rather than *doing*. Feeling connected to our highest Self is quite a challenge when we are constantly rushing around, busying ourselves with work, family, friends, emails, TV and all the other distractions. When was the last time you stopped rushing around and sat still in quiet contemplation?

I cannot tell you about *your* connection to the indwelling presence of God. I can only tell you about my experience and about the things I do to become more accident prone and to increase my chances of having, what I call, a mystical experience. If you want to feel, sense, see and know who you really are, and how connected you are to all Life, it is important to become okay with being alone with yourself in the silence.

If the idea of being alone with yourself, in silence, caused you to stop breathing, please take a breath. It is possible that the idea of being alone with yourself, without **any** distractions or noise, is a daunting concept. Many of us use our busy lives to avoid doing the very things this book invites. And yet when we stop *doing* and become willing to *be*, that is the point when the door opens to a higher awareness of who we are.

Almost every world faith has a mystical tradition filled with seekers wanting to experience their personal connection with the Divine. One of my personal favourites is Rumi. He lived in Persia during the 13 century and was a Sufi mystic, poet and theologian. His poetry speaks of love and oneness with all things in the most beautiful terms, and reading his work can be another way I remember who I really am.

> *"Your task is not to seek for love, but merely to seek and find*
> *all the barriers within yourself that you have built against it."*
>
> ~ RUMI

The concept of a 'Mystical Experience' may be strange to you, and perhaps you have never thought about such a thing before. I didn't really think about it until after I experienced my first one. I was taking part in a guided process called 'Visioning' at a weekend conference many years ago. The process is widely used to connect with a high vision for your life, or a particular project. It's a bit like a guided meditation mixed with self-enquiry questions and I have always found it to be a very powerful process. On this occasion our group had been guided into the first question, "What is the high idea for my life?" Almost immediately I felt loved, held, supported and cherished with an intensity that I still have no words for. These feelings were overwhelmingly beautiful, rich and deep. Something within me opened in a new way. It was almost as if the part of me that identifies as 'Juliet Vorster' vanished. I felt consumed by this radiant tsunami of emotion and I felt what I would describe as the 'Love of God'. That feeling came from deep within my being and has never left me. I sometimes forget, but with very little effort, I am able to reconnect.

Had I not been in that process, I could not have had that

experience. Again, returning to the message in the story, I do my spiritual practice so that I may increase my chances of connecting that deeply to Love and Oneness, to become more "accident prone". I have found in my own life that as I experience these fleeting moments of profound mystical and spiritual realisation, I am inspired and motivated to keep seeking and releasing all the barriers within me that cause a false belief in separation.

Lean into the discomfort, allow yourself to float

Allowing yourself to open to these possibilities requires surrender. Letting go of who you think you are and allowing a fresh opening of awareness can be somewhat frightening. And yet when you do it, when you let go of clinging to all you know, it is quite remarkable how easy it can be to float.

In the first chapter of his book *Illusions*, Richard Bach tells a story about a group of creatures who live clinging to the river bottom. Eventually one of these creatures decides he cannot possibly live by clinging to this small existence. Despite the opinions of his fellows, he releases his hold. Once in the current, along his journey he discovers this:

"The river delights to lift us free,
if only we dare let go."

We are so much more than this fragile carbon suitcase that we identify with. Our true essence is an extract of the wholeness of life, we are each individualised expressions of God or Source or Universal Energy or what ever words work for you. We are never separated from our Source or from every other thing, creature, and person on the planet. There is only one thing, and we're all it. Remember the analogy of the ocean and the drop. As a single drop you have all of the ocean within you, but you, alone, are not all of the ocean.

You are in the ocean of Life. Rather than clinging to what you have always known, are you willing to let go and allow the river of Life to lift you free? You can't let go a bit, just as a woman can't be a bit pregnant, you either continue clinging or you release your hold and surrender into what comes next. As you release you may have a few bumps and knocks, but the more you let go of struggle and resistance, the easier it is to float. Life is supposed to be much easier than we allow it to be. When we let go of our need to control everything and direct the outcomes, when we stop avoiding deeper self enquiry, then a space is created for something so much richer to unfold.

There is a light within you. It can never be extinguished or diminished. It is the spark of life, your Divine Essence, the truth of who you really are. It's time to rediscover your light and let it shine. Another Sufi mystic, Hafiz, says it all in this poem.

> *You are the Sun in drag.*
> *You are God hiding from yourself.*
> *Remove all the 'mine' - that is the veil.*
> *Why ever worry about anything?*
> *Listen to what your friend Hafiz knows for certain:*
> *The appearance of this world*
> *Is a Magi's brilliant trick, though its affairs are*
> *Nothing into nothing.*
> *You are a divine elephant with amnesia*
> *Trying to live in an ant hole.*
> *Sweetheart, O sweetheart*
> *You are God in Drag!*
>
> ~ HAFIZ

I invite you to contemplate how it might be that *you are a divine elephant with amnesia trying to live in an ant hole?* Let go of what is and allow your *greatest yet to be* to lift you into the current and set you free. Allow the richness of your imagination to engage with the image of an elephant trying to live in an ant hole. Are there any areas in your life where you are playing small, putting yourself down, or living from a belief that you are 'less than' or 'not enough' in some way? You are an expression of source energy, you are a divine elephant, who has forgotten just how amazing you really are. It's time to remember.

Chapter 13 - Awareness Exercise - Developing your connection

Regardless of your personal spiritual beliefs, developing your personal connection to that greater something within yourself is a valuable exercise to expand your intuition and increase your self awareness.

Read through this guided journey and then close your eyes and allow your imagination to lead you. You may also want to read it aloud and record your own voice, then listen as you journey.

- Take a deep breath and as you release, imagine letting go of everything. Relax your shoulders and release any tension you are holding in your body. Keep breathing, releasing and relaxing as you allow your body to become more and more relaxed.

- Bring your awareness to the middle of your chest, within your body. Imagine in this space there is a glowing ball of radiant light pulsing out waves of unconditional love. Allow yourself to feel, sense and experience the warmth, peace and compassion that this light radiates through your being.

- Play with imagining the light getting a little bigger, and a little bigger, and also recognise that no matter how you might try, you cannot make it disappear or go out.

- As you connect to this radiance within you, allow the light to melt away all fear, doubt, guilt, blame and shame. Allow it to dissolve any thoughts or feelings of 'less than' or 'not enough'. Embrace a deeper feeling of love, support, acceptance, care and kindness for yourself. Be willing to grow these feelings; fill your body with a visceral knowing of these sensations and then imagine radiating them out into the world.

- As you become more illuminated from within, imagine meeting other people and seeing their inner light radiating out in bright streams of glittering colour. As your rich and fertile imagination lets go of what is and awakens a new possibility for living, imagine your individualised Self melting into one with all that you see. Be open to a greater experience of Life as you breathe into this indwelling presence, whilst simultaneously becoming aware that it is all around you.

- Rest here, in this imaginisation, for as long as you like. Bathe in the feeling of connection and oneness. Allow the feelings and sensations to fill you up fully. Remember to keep breathing.

When you feel ready to return, take a deep breath and reconnect with your environment.

Once you have started to open to this deeper awareness of your inner light it gets easier and easier to recognise the presence in any situation. And just like all the other exercises in this book, it is all about awareness and practise.

You will get the best results in your own life if you actually **do** the exercises and create the space in your own life to become more accident prone.

One last thing: Even if your beliefs are being challenged by this chapter I invite you to just be willing.

Take a moment to write down any realisation you received during this process.

What's God Got To Do With It?

Chapter 14

GET READY TO FLY

"Perfectionism is not the same thing as striving to be our best. Perfectionism is not about healthy achievement and growth; it's a shield."

~ BRENÉ BROWN

We have come to the final chapter together and I think, perhaps, we have the same question: what comes next? My hours of writing have brought together information and ideas, and this book is the result. It is my passionate hope that it will awaken something fresh in your life. But how much use will it be, as you close the pages and put it on the shelf, if you don't take any action? My intention in writing this book is that it might be a catalyst to ignite something greater within you. It is filled with practical tools and processes that you can apply in your life. I have shared all this so that you are equipped with sufficient knowledge to enable you to experience greater peace, poise and prosperity in your life.

This book is not designed to be a measure or yardstick for how well you are doing in life. It is designed to help you review the thoughts you think and the beliefs you hold so that you can liberate a new realisation about who you are and how you can live a more thriving life in every regard. Let go of the need to be perfect, to get it right, and to measure up to anyone else. You are your unique Self. You are an expression of something greater, some infinite conscious intelligence that already had everything figured out before you arrived.

> *"Fear is the cheapest room in the house, I would like to see*
> *you living in better conditions."*
>
> ~ HAFIZ

Now is the time to get out of your head, stop thinking about doing or not doing, and start being who you are here to be. It's time to shine your light and let go of all the beliefs that have held you back and kept you playing a small game. Now is the time to ignite your success by moving beyond your beliefs. To really get things moving, now is the time for action.

How many books have you read, workshops have you attended, webinars and tele-seminars have you listened to? If you are anything like me, it's quite a few. Now think about all the things you learned and all the wisdom you were exposed to. Also like me, you may have not taken quite as much action as you could have, or as you wished you had. I know we all get busy and we forget to put ourselves as a priority. Let's make today different. Let's join together and decide that we are worthy and we deserve to ignite success beyond beliefs just for us. I know everyone around us benefits as we grow in consciousness, but let's take the journey for our own delight.

There is a great deal of ground covered in this book and it can take time to absorb it all. A bit like our earlier conversation about the stew, it's okay for you to take time to expand your consciousness to the next level of awareness. Be gentle with yourself and be willing to value yourself enough to take the action steps.

I hold my own knowing for the truth of who you are, but I would love to see you living an even more thriving life. I know you will have picked up some great ideas and probably spent a little time thinking about how they could impact your life. But my wish for you is that you embody these ideas and you apply the principles so that

you actually make changes and experience something different.
You already learned C+B=A. Now it's time for your ABC:

"Awareness Builds Consciousness."

~ DENNIS MERRITT JONES

Throughout this book there have been different exercises designed to build awareness. I invite you to complete these exercises so that you become more aware of your thoughts and beliefs. As you get to know yourself more, you are better able to be selective about what works and what doesn't in your life. In my own life, and working with clients, I have seen lives transformed once limiting beliefs have been discovered and released. Awareness is the discovery process. Once you become aware, you are naturally shifting your consciousness, changing your beliefs and rewiring your mind. That can happen as quickly as the awareness is revealed and, sometimes it takes a while. I haven't managed to create a formula for that yet, mainly because we are each unique and come to our own realisations at the perfect moment for us.

In the UK we play a game called Pooh Sticks. It comes from A.A. Milne's Winnie The Pooh stories. You need some people, each with a stick, then you need a stream or small river and preferably a bridge, although the bridge is not essential. At an appointed moment everyone drops their stick into the river, and the race begins. Whoever's stick gets to the appointed finish line first is the winner. This can be from one side of a bridge to the other. The relevant thing about Pooh Sticks is that sometimes a stick gets caught up in the bank or on a sandbar. All that is needed to get the stick back in the flow of the water is a little nudge. Because I really want you to get in the flow of igniting success beyond beliefs in your life, I am here to give you a little nudge.

Let's get started

Be willing to let this be more fun than you think. The best way to implement changes in your life, that stick and last the test of time, is to make the changes fun. If the idea of 'practise' sounds boring or difficult or time-consuming, you won't do it. So the most important priority is to take the first step and make it fun. I can't tell you what that is for you, so here are some starting places. You don't have to do them all, read through them and decide which would be the most fun for you. Just pick one and get started in the flow:

1. Put a picture that symbolises your ideal life in your line of sight as the first thing you see when you wake up. This will remind you that you are making changes. You could even write on it, "I am willing to change."

2. Before you get started with your day, sit up in bed, or go to a comfy chair and breathe consciously for three to five minutes. The aim is to get to ten minutes, but just for now, start with what you can manage. *Something* is better than *nothing*.

3. Either with your family or a group of like-minded people, book some time each week to share what you are grateful for. Make it a fun thing to do. To help you along with this you can download a free gratitude journal from my website: www.JulietVorster.com/GratitudeJournal.

4. Take a five minute walk at lunch time. Remember this is about getting started, not completing a marathon. As you walk, be mindful and aware of your surroundings, and allow your mind to become a little quieter. This will better enable you to hear the still, small voice of your inspiration.

5. Make a list of things that bring you joy and read it every day. You can even add to it as you start to notice more things.

6. Find some pictures that inspire you to remember your inner light, such as a beautiful sunset, a baby (human or animal), a flickering candle, anything that inspires you. Even if you are not sure you have one yet. Cut out some pictures and make a little collage of them. Put them where you will notice them regularly.

These are just starting points. Points of action so that you can build momentum and start to notice the things changing in your life. Remember the 3Ps of Practise, Persistence and Patience. The way you have been thinking, the beliefs you have been operating from and the actions you have been taking as a result have been programmed deep into your belief system. To unpick and reprogram them can be an instant thing or something that takes a little more time. Allow yourself to go at your pace and resist the urge to change everything instantly.

Success Qualities

> *"To know even one life has breathed easier because you have lived. This is to have succeeded."*
>
> ~ RALPH WALDO EMERSON

Let us return to our discussion of success from the beginning of this book. There may be many ways in which you can declare yourself successful in the world of things. But what about inner success? What feelings would you want to experience to consider yourself successful from the inside out? Would it be peace, happiness, love, appreciation, a combination of these, a single one or something completely different? Take a moment right now to make a list of five feelings that you identify as emotions you experience when you are feeling successful from within.

Evolution from within

Early on in this book I proposed the idea that you are already successful, that you have an innate essence that cannot be created or destroyed - the part of you that is more than the carbon atoms your suitcase is created from. Your whole Self is something that is not at the whim of external opinion, social mores, the stock market, physical health or the weather. As you build and develop your personal connection with your inner essence, you will discover that the appearance of things in the outer world of effects starts to change. The things you put high value on when you started may become less important. The everyday things you took for granted may gain greater significance. Any number of physical things start to change when you change the inner landscape of your beliefs and thoughts.

Keep moving, change is constant

Your perceptions of external things change as you realise that the story you made up about their meaning in your life has evaporated. Step by step you will become more present and mindful of what you are thinking, the stories you are making up and the beliefs that are attached to those thoughts. As that happens, release any need for judgement and criticism, of yourself or others, and imagine yourself playing in a stream of water. As much as you splash and jump in the water, you cannot stop the flow. It is the stream's purpose to flow and it is your mind's purpose to think. You will not stop the thinking, but, with practise, you will stop believing all that you think.

Practise

Now that you are acquainted with the five foundational principles, the next step to igniting success beyond beliefs is to get started with the first of the 3Ps - Practise. In every chapter there have been exercises, self-enquiry questions and practical tools to enable you to move beyond your beliefs. The more you apply, review and redo those exercises, the easier it will be for you to change your thinking and liberate the beliefs that no longer serve you. Perhaps the first practice you could implement is conscious breathing. Take a breath and connect with your body.

It is important that you don't let feeling overwhelmed create inaction. If you feel that there are too many areas of your life where you want to experience change and greater success, just for now, pick one. Don't try to do them all at once. If you think every area of your life needs some attention, then take a moment to create a priority list. You can do that right now:

My Igniting Success Priority List

1. _____

2. _____

3. _____

4. _____

5. _____

You will discover that as you apply the basic principles from the first section of the book to one area of your life, the changes will act on every area. What one particular challenge currently active in your life would make you feel much better about yourself if you experienced a shift in it? It doesn't have to be the biggest thing, just pick one and get started.

When you start applying the principles to a specific situation or challenge in your life, first remember to be gentle with yourself and do your best to stay away from judgement, criticism and blame. (That, in its self, is a practice). Let's run through an imaginary example and see how it might reveal in daily practice:

Issue: I never have enough time to get everything done and I'm permanently exhausted.

Step-by-step inquiry

Foundation 1: My thoughts and beliefs create my experience. - Make some time throughout the week to contemplate and journal (write about) the answers to these and similar questions.

- What do I believe about my worth and value?
- Do I have a story that says I have to produce/deliver certain results in order to be worthy?
- Am I constantly seeking to be perfect so that others will approve of me?
- What do I believe about 'my way' of doing things? Am I stuck thinking no-one can do things to my standard?
- Do I have a belief that says something like, 'busy equals valuable or important?'
- What do I think it would mean about me if I sat and relaxed for thirty minutes in the middle of the day?

Foundation 2: My imagination is powerful and I can use it to change my experience. - Instead of worrying and living in the future or the past whilst doing all the chores, use your mind for good by imagining some different scenarios.

Could I imagine having a day where I don't have to rush, I have time to do the things I love, no-one puts pressure on me to 'be here' or 'do this'?

Could I imagine feeling a sense of self-worth from within that was not dependent on anyone else's opinion? What would that look and feel like?

Could I imagine letting go of the need to be perfect? What would that look and feel like?

Could I imagine getting to the evening and having time to sit and do something relaxing without the need for a glass of wine to chill me out?

Foundation 3: My feelings are rocket fuel for my mental creations. - It is valuable to bring both your emotion-based feelings and your physical sense-based feelings into your new creation. As you move through the enquiry questions and imaginisations, be sure to add the feeling tones to the practice.

What would it feel like on the inside to be rested and peaceful?

If I spent a couple of hours doing something just for me that I love and want to do, what would that sound like, what would my hands be doing, and what would it look like?

If I were to let go of feeling guilty about taking a break, what would the sense of freedom and release feel like within me?

Foundation 4: I am co-creating with everyone else in the conscious collective Mind. - Remember you are not living in a bubble. You are in this world with seven billion others, all of whom are expressing their thoughts and beliefs into the collective mind field. You are also tapped in to the infinite intelligence. Anything you are seeking is available to you through the collective mind. Use foundation 4 to deepen your awareness of others around you and check in with any stories you are making up.

Perhaps you have a belief that goes like this, 'my partner is lazy and doesn't pull his/her weight around the house.' Did you ever stop to ask them to help out? Or perhaps ask why they don't help out as much. The answer may be something like this, 'What's the point of me doing anything when you come behind me and do it your way?'

Check in with the beliefs and behaviours you saw modelled as you grew up. What influence have other people's view points on self-worth, productivity and doing things a certain way had on your belief system?

Allow your mind to get quiet and connect to the indwelling source and the infinite intelligence of universal mind. Then ask yourself, "What one thing can I do to bring me a greater sense of peace right now?"

Foundation 5: 3Ps of Practise, Persistence and Patience. - Always take the time to be patient with yourself as you start to apply these principles and be persistent with your practise.

Take time every day to breathe consciously. Start with just a few minutes and build up to a full ten. There is a crazy sounding paradox which has great scientific study behind it: When you are rested, relaxed and happy you become more productive and better at creating inspired solutions to problems.

Practise being okay with who you are. Be willing to accept yourself just as you are.

Say 'no' to at least one thing each week that you really don't want to do; be willing to let go of the need to feel guilty or to explain yourself when you say no.

Remember that an empty well can't quench anyone's thirst. With the space you created by saying 'no', do something that fills you up from the inside out.

In addition to these five foundational ideas, I have introduced a number of tools throughout the book. Trust your own inner guidance to inspire you to practise the ones that will empower the greatest shifts within you and your life. Always remembering that there is no fundamental right or wrong, good or bad. Each situation is part of your life journey and each tool will have its uses in different ways and at different times. Just like only focussing on one specific area of your life, you don't need to use every tool all at once. Trust your inner wisdom to direct you to the perfect process in each situation.

This is a brief set of suggestions to one imaginary situation. It offers some ideas for the   practical application of the five foundations. Your situations and challenges are going to be unique to you but hopefully this gives some insight to how you might apply them to your life.

Persistence

The second step in creating success beyond beliefs is persistence. The principles and tools presented in this book are not designed as a one hit fix or an instant cure. They are foundations for a different way of living. Much like the difference between going on a three month crash diet or deciding to fundamentally change what and how you eat and nourish yourself. These concepts are a way of life. They are a choice.

Setting your intention to change the way you live your life is a powerfully transformative decision. And sometimes you will forget that you set the intention and you will slip back into the old thoughts and beliefs. If that happens, just be gentle with yourself and get back on track when you remember. As you create new habits and set fresh intentions, you may sometimes slip back; in those moments just remember to breathe. It doesn't mean that you are not destined to change your beliefs, it simply means the old programming hasn't yet been cleared out completely.

Changing your beliefs and your way of thinking can happen

very quickly; in an instant, in fact. For example, you may have washed your dishes by hand for as long as you lived in the house, but once the dishwasher is installed you rarely wash even a cup by hand. Perhaps you may have the odd moment when you forget you have a dishwasher and start filling the sink with water, but soon enough you'll remember and go back to stacking the dishes in the machine. Change doesn't have to be a struggle, unless you want it to be. Choosing new beliefs and ways of thinking quickly become habits when you practise the new thoughts and behaviours persistently, and allow the process of life to unfold through you without making yourself wrong, bad or less than when you momentarily forget.

Patience: The art of letting go of wanting it now

The final P in the 3Ps model is Patience. Even if you are quickly able to make changes to your thinking, weed out the old beliefs and stop making up stories about yourself and life in general, it may take a little while for things in the world of form and stuff to change visibly. Once again this is not a reason to declare that these ideas don't work or that you are not destined to have a better life.

Sometimes things come in an instant and some times they come a little slower. Think of it like making a good stew. Sticking all the ingredients in a microwave and zapping them for ten minutes is not going to make the tastiest stew even though all the ingredients are fully cooked. The art of a good stew is allowing it the time, in a medium/low oven to, well not to state the obvious, but to *stew*. The slow process of gentle cooking releases all the flavours and juices, allowing a wonderful infusion of tastes as well as delivering meat and vegetables that are melt-in-the-mouth tender.

If things aren't changing quite as quickly as you'd love them to, think of your life as a delicious stew, slowly cooking down into something soft and tender with beautiful aromatic flavours and mouth-tingling tastes. In my experience, it's worth waiting for. In the age of ready meals and instant text chat, waiting patiently is becoming a lost art. In the case of personal transformation it's a practice that you may want to be willing to embrace, even if it feels difficult. I still have the occasional moment of metaphorically stamping my feet at the Universe when things don't yet look like I want them to, but I have learned to trust the process. I have gained my own body of evidence that tells me the greater intelligence of life has everything covered, I just need to be willing to let it in.

> *"Beliefs have the power to create and the power to destroy.*
> *Human beings have the awesome ability to take any*
> *experience of their lives and create a meaning that*
> *disempowers them or one that can literally save their lives."*
>
> ~ TONY ROBBINS

Changing what you believe is the key to changing your life. It is the very essence of igniting success beyond beliefs. As humans, we have the innate ability (a natural inner capacity) to be objective, to be the observer of our life. Typically we have been taught to use that ability to compare, measure and judge ourselves and almost always separate ourselves from others by being more than or less than. You now have tools and knowledge to objectively review the beliefs you hold about life and your place within it. These allow you to compassionately let go of the beliefs that no longer serve you and become willing to embrace new thoughts about what is possible and how successful you can be in the world.

Everything is in divine right order

There is an intelligence that has the world rotating around the sun, it has gravity keeping us stuck to the planet, and has the sun's warmth and light creating a biosphere that sustains human life. That is all going on, even whilst you are asleep. You may find a sense of relief when you come to recognise, regardless of anything you may name it, that there is an intelligent consciousness, greater than we are yet expressing through us, that has everything handled already. You can stop trying to push the waves and change the tides by the force of your mind or your body. You can step back, trust the process of life and live in the flow.

Once you recognise this, then you can embrace the fact that you are the creator of your life. Through your powerful thoughts and feelings you can imagine into being anything you would love to experience. Not through force, but through allowing the natural flow. Using your thoughts as the steering wheel and your feelings as the engine, you can steer your life wherever you wish. As you come to realise these essential truths, or governing principles, you naturally become more relaxed, calm and peaceful because you are resting in that greater Mind. As you surrender into the natural flow, you can change the thought you are thinking in any moment and, as a result, change the experience you are having.

Always remember that every other being on this planet is also using their mind within the Infinite Mind and we don't all want the same life experience. That is not good or bad, it's simply a different expression. You may love horror movies, and I may love Disney cartoons. That doesn't mean anything about either of us other than we like different movies. This thing called 'free will' allows us all to choose the movies we play out in our lives. One is not better than or worse than any other. We are all unique expressions of the Infinite Intelligence and in our uniqueness we are all the same. Be okay with your movie choices so far and be willing to change them if you no longer enjoy what they offer. Every experience you have had has shaped you into the magnificent person you are today. (Yes, I really mean that you are magnificent).

No-one has arrived on this planet as a mistake. Each one of us is here with a purpose, for a purpose and on a purpose. Mine is to awaken you to who you really are. What's yours? You may not know yet, but I am certain that you do have purpose. This infinite intelligence that keeps all the planets moving without crashing and orchestrates the mysteries of the universe doesn't make mistakes, and that includes you. No matter what has happened to you in your life and regardless of anything you may have done, you are one with this thing called Life, you are spectacular and you are here for a reason.

I forgot to mention the fourth P

Even though, until now, we have only talked about the magic 3Ps, I am concluding this book and sending you back into the world with a fourth P - Purpose. I invite you to open a space of willingness within you to know that you have a purpose for being here. Once you have opened to that new idea, allow your rich and fertile imagination to get started on what your purpose may be. What do you love? What lights you up from the inside? What is the thing you would do for free all day long if you didn't have to make money to eat and pay rent?

Why is it so valuable to discover your purpose? I believe that when we get clear about our purpose it impels us forward with such clarity and passion that life feels like we are simply floating through every day. Even though the ups and downs of life still happen, living a life of purpose enables a different perspective. I have found that stress, worry and fear have become things of a dim and distant past now that I have discovered and fully embraced my purpose.

Greater self-awareness is a great help in discovering your purpose. As you come to better know and understand yourself and your life journey, it is probable that increased clarity will inspire you to recognise your purpose. If you are still not sure why or for what reason you are here, my friend and mentor Dennis Merritt Jones is the person to connect with. His purpose is to guide other people to discover their purpose. Dennis has been hugely influential in my life and I know he can add value in your life too. He is an award-winning author and you can find out all about him at www.DennisMerrittJones.com. Remember to tell him I sent you.

On a very practical level, the discovery of my purpose has allowed me to finally write this book that I have been procrastinating about for at least seven years. Your purpose may not become the economic engine for your life, but it will become the reason you greet each new day with delight and expectancy. Every morning I say to myself, "I expect a spectacular day." And I can assure you, my life gets better and better with each new dawn.

Trust that the infinite intelligence within you knows your purpose - you have simply been acting as the *divine elephant with amnesia trying to live in an ant hole*. As you apply the self-enquiry questions and the awareness exercises in your life you will certainly start to discover new information, about yourself, your beliefs and how your thinking has affected your life so far.

Remember your history does not predict your destiny. You are the only thinker in your mind and your mind is connected to the universal mind. Everything you need to know is already directly connected to you, in you and through you. It is simply in the process of allowing, trusting and practising that you will embrace and embody this new way of thinking and these new beliefs. As you do that you can't help but ignite success beyond beliefs.

I see you and I know who you really are. You and I are one in this infinite intelligence and I hold you in love as you break out from the cocoon of old beliefs and take flight on the radiant wings of your essential magnificence. I look forward to sharing the sky with you on this journey of life.

With all my love, Juliet

RESOURCES

We are blessed to live in a world where information is widely available and easily accessible, this can lead to an occasional sense of overwhelm. As I have sometimes been described as an information tsunami, especially when I give a live presentation, I am keen to ensure that you don't feel overloaded, but that you feel supported for the steps ahead. My best advice, when it comes to seeking your next step, is to trust your own inner knowing. You are the only expert on you, so tune in and feel what comes next on your journey.

Books

- *You Can Heal Your Life* - Louise L. Hay
- *You'll See It When You Believe It* - Wayne W. Dyer
- *Your Erroneous Zones* - Wayne W. Dyer
- *Change Your Thoughts - Change Your Life* - Wayne W. Dyer
- *What You Think Of Me Is None Of My Business* - Terry Cole Whittaker
- *The Gifts Of Imperfection* - Brené Brown
- *Daring Greatly* - Brené Brown
- *Creative Visualization* - Shakti Gawain
- *Ordering From The Cosmic Kitchen* - Patricia Crane
- *Who Do You Think You Are?* - Rick Nichols
- *The Go-Giver* - Bob Burg and John David Mann
- *Power vs Force* - David R. Hawkins
- *Code to Joy* - George Pratt & Peter Lambrou
- *The Art of Being* - Dennis Merritt Jones
- *The Art of Uncertainty* - Dennis Merritt Jones
- *Feel The Fear and Do It Anyway* - Susan Jeffers
- *The Money Keys* - Karen Russo

- *The Happiness Advantage* - Shawn Achor
- *The Inside-Out Revolution* - Michael Neill
- *Feel Happy Now* - Michael Neill
- *Feeling Is The Secret* - Neville Goddard
- *The Biology of Belief* - Bruce Lipton
- *The Prophet* - Khalil Gibran

Films

- What The Bleep Do We Know?
- The Secret
- Fat, Sick, and Nearly Dead
- Forks Over Knives
- Food Matters
- Crazy Sexy Cancer
- People V. The State of Illusion

Web

- TED.com
- HeartMath.org
- DennisMerrittJones.com
- TheMoneyKeys.com
- NewThoughtConference.com
- JulietVorster.com

ABOUT JULIET

Juliet is a seeker and student first. She has been looking for answers to the big questions in life for as long as she can remember. This inquisitive nature has led her to many grand adventures in life; each one helping to shape her into the woman she is constantly becoming.

Passionate about being the best she can be, Juliet has developed many tools and processes to empower and enable people to awaken to their own innate magnificence and worth. Being fully committed to these concepts, she consistently applies and practices them in her own life.

Trained in many spiritual, metaphysical and holistic modalities, Juliet synthesises what she learns and transmits it in a way that is easy to understand and practical to apply in everyday life. She seeks to serve the world by teaching simple tools that allow us to rise above the doubts and fears of our inner voice. Juliet believes that anyone and everyone can move beyond their current circumstances and beliefs - if they choose to; and thus step into the upward spiral of their greatest yet to be.

Juliet currently lives in Hampshire, England with her wife, Mary, and with white cat Monty and black cat Charcoal. She describes the cats as the yin and yang of her life. She travels extensively presenting workshops, inspirational talks and retreats, and is available for one to one coaching, corporate consultancy, keynote talks and guest appearances worldwide.

Notes